SAY IT WITH QUILTS

Diana McClun
&
Laura Nownes

Copyright © 1997 Diana McClun and Laura Nownes
Developmental Editor: Barbara Konzak Kuhn
Technical Editor: Joyce Engels Lytle
Cover Design: John Cram, Kathy Lee, and Diana McClun
Book Design: Kajun Graphics
Illustrator: Kandy Petersen
All photography by Sharon Risedorph unless otherwise noted.

Library of Congress Cataloging-in-Publication Data
McClun, Diana, date.
　　Say it with quilts / Diana McClun and Laura Nownes.
　　　　　　　　p.　　　cm.
　　Includes index.
　　ISBN 1-57120-023-1
　　1. Patchwork quilts. 2. Patchwork—Patterns.
I. Nownes, Laura,date.　　　II. Title.
TT835.M3994　　1997
746.46'041—dc20　　　　　　　　　　　　　　　　96-38606
　　　　　　　　　　　　　　　　　　　　　　　　　　CIP

Ruler designs Copyright 1986, 1995, Omnigrid®, Inc. All rights reserved.
U.S. Patent. 4,779,346; Ca. Pat. 1,297,286

Liberty is a registered trademark of Liberty of London Prints Limited.

Published by C&T Publishing
P.O. Box 1456
Lafayette, California 94549

Printed in the United States of America
10 9 8 7 6 5 4 3 2 1

Table of Contents

Preface

IN THE HEART OF THE BAY AREA, outside San Francisco, California, a legendary exhibit is a special showing of quilt art by a noted local quilt-maker. This artist displays her yearly accomplishments at a gallery showing, and the number of quilts is always impressive. After one visit, I returned home curious to count my year's work. How did I stack up? I counted my fingers quickly recalling each experience, each event, and each quilt. I had worked on several quilts for brides, a few more for new babies, some for birthdays, one for a going away party, and one for a retirement celebration. Yet, not one of these quilts did I own. At that moment my personal output became less important than the realization of my reason for quiltmaking: giving gifts of love to others. My quiltmaking commemorates other people's lives and the special people in my life with honored events.

—Diana McClun

OVER THE YEARS AS A QUILTMAKER, I have made many quilts. Some were made specifically for inclusion in books and others for special people and the memorable events in their lives. But the most exciting and rewarding quilts I have ever made are those that were made with a special person in mind. While working on the quilts for close friends, I was filled with thoughts of love and the relationships we shared. These feelings, coupled with the surprise element and anticipation of presenting it to them, made the experiences exciting for me. That's what this book is all about…our feelings toward a special person, event, pattern, or fabric that inspires the making of our quilts.

—Laura Nownes

The Quilts

JOHN KEATES WROTE, "A thing of beauty is a joy forever." When this external, intangible quality is expressed through the art of quiltmaking, it rewards both the quilter and recipient with pleasurable feelings and deep satisfaction for days, months, and even years after the project is complete. Quilters may create one, two, three, or more quilts just to feel this force, which propels them to continue reaching for the surprised joy.

This book focuses on ideas, patterns, personal vision, individual style, and the experiences that comprise the quiltmaking scene. Each quilt in this book allows the creator an opportunity to transmit a personal, special message. Some quilters find inspiration from chaos in their lives with piles of fabric stacked everywhere; others listen to the rhythm and harmony of the sewing machine for serenity. Searching for just the right pattern and hunting for the correct palette of colors in the fabric often creates excitement and inspiration. Quilting provides the creator with an opportunity for renewing friendships, enjoying another's company, or expressing their personality through home decorating. Using quilts for decorating walls and beds allows endless pleasure and feelings of well-being.

For some quilters, this creative process permits time for solace, peace, or closure to life's problems. Gifts, tokens of caring on special occasions, whether joyous or sad, teach us many of life's little lessons about loving and caring. Quiltmaking provides an opportunity to listen to ourselves and express our joys or heartaches through the threads of the fabric. Quilts reflect the ambitions, hobbies, employment, or other unique attributes of the giver or receiver. Loved quilts are the owner's personal signature. Each quiltmaker, through the sharing of hands and hearts, can feel the special excitement, the possible surprised joy.

Sweet Dreams Sara

LAURA'S STORY

My older daughter Sara's need for a new bed covering gave me the opportunity to engage in one of my favorite pastimes: making quilts. But what was more appealing to me was the opportunity to work with my daughter. Together we had fun deciding on the pattern and color, and then searching for just the right fabrics. First, we chose the X-quisite pattern because it creates a beautiful repeat design and also lends itself to the use of many scraps. Next, the color choice was an obvious one: Sara's favorite color is blue (although, I always think of Sara's sparkling blue eyes). Finally, we had the most fun sifting through bags of scraps for the many blue and white pieces. Now this quilt covers us both as we cuddle together, sharing special moments and reading bedtime stories.

Sara, I hope this quilt always covers you with love and warmth, and may all your dreams be sweet ones.—LOVE, *MOM*

Sweet Dreams Sara
by the authors

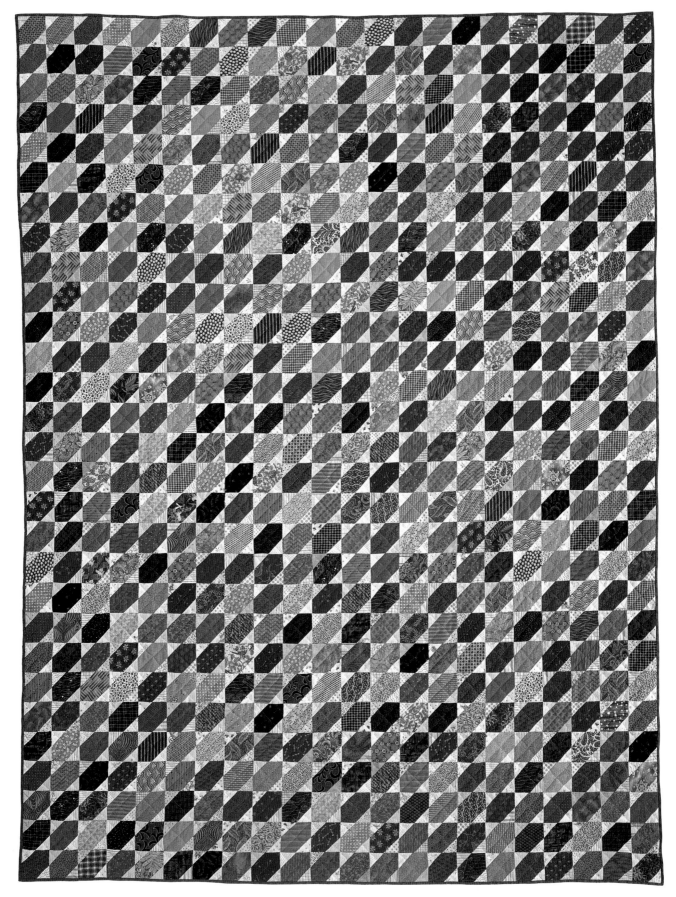

Traditional block pattern: X-quisite; quilted by Anna Venti

X-quisite block

FINISHED SIZE	66½″ x 87½″
BLOCKS SET	22 x 29
X-QUISITE BLOCKS: TOTAL	638

Yardage

Light colors: fabrics to total…**3 ⅝**
Medium and dark colors: fabrics to total…**5 ½**
Backing…**5 ¼**
Binding: ¼″ wide, finished…**½**

Cutting

Blocks

Light colors:
    (A) 2″-wide strips…**61** *Cut strips into 2″ squares—need 1,276.*
Medium and dark colors:
    (B) 3½″-wide strips…**54** *Cut strips into 3½″ squares—need 638.*

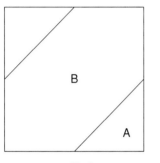

3″ block

Backing and Binding

Backing: lengths…**2**
    See piecing diagram (page 116) **A**
Binding: width…**1⅞″**

Construction

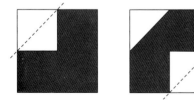

Step 1

1. Use the double half-square triangle technique to attach the light squares (A) to the medium and dark squares (B), as shown. Refer to Part 2 (page 108) for help, if needed.
2. Arrange the blocks. Then sew the blocks together in a straight set (page 111) to complete the quilt top.

Can You Find Your Pet?

DR. DAVID McCLUN, Diana's
husband and a veterinarian, dedicated this quilt to all the owners,
both children and adults, whose pets
have received his medical care. A
collection of cats, dogs, and birds,
printed on the fabrics, highlight the
quilt and reflect his personal love of
animals. The quilt represents a bed
of softness and caring, which is the
basis of David's help and healing.
Can you find your pet?

Can You Find Your Pet?
by the authors

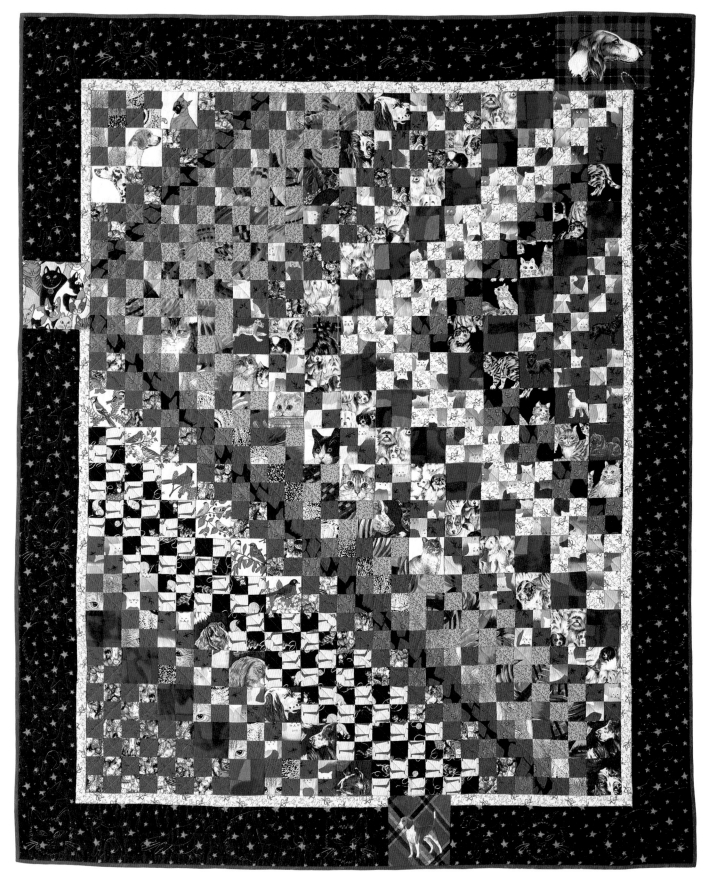

Traditional block pattern: Four-Patch; machine quilted by Kathy Sandbach

FINISHED SIZE	57″ x 69″
BLOCKS SET	15 x 19
FOUR-PATCH BLOCKS: TOTAL	203
PLAIN BLOCKS: TOTAL	82

Yardage

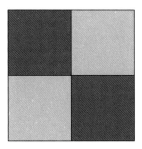

Four-Patch block

Four-Patch blocks: fourteen fabrics, *each*…**¼**

Plain blocks (includes large border blocks): fabrics to total…**1**

Inner border:

   Crosswise…**⅜**

   or lengthwise…**1¾**

Outer border:

   Crosswise…**1¼**

   or lengthwise…**2**

Backing…**3½**

Binding: ¼″ wide, finished…**½**

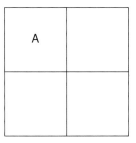

3″ block

Cutting

Blocks

Four-Patch blocks:

   (A) 2″-wide strips, *each*…**3**

Plain blocks:

   (B) 3½″-wide strips…**7** *Cut strips into 3½″ squares—need 82.*

Borders, Backing, and Binding

Large Pet Blocks for border…**3** (size determined by fabric print)

Inner border: width…**1½″**

Outer border: width…**5¼″**

Backing: lengths…**2**

   See piecing diagram (page 116) **B**

Binding: width…**1⅞″**

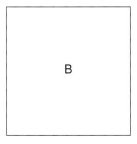

3″ block

Construction

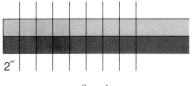

Step 1

1. Organize seven combinations of fabrics for Four-Patch blocks. Sew the strips together in sets of two. Then cut the sets apart every 2″, as shown.
2. Block sew order: see diagram.
3. Arrange the Four-Patch and Plain blocks together, using the diagram as a guide; or, create your own design. Then sew all of the blocks together in a straight set (page 111).
4. Sew the inner and outer border strips together lengthwise.
5. At random, join the large Pet blocks to the border, incorporating the blocks into the border design and cutting the border strips where necessary.
6. Attach the border strips to complete the quilt top. Refer to Part 2 (page 114) for help, if needed.

Step 2

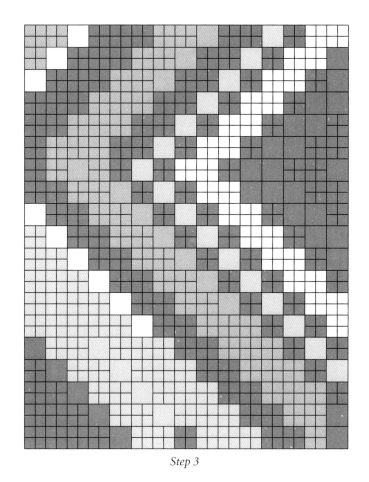

Step 3

Sunny and Hazy

FOR REBECCA ROHRKASTE, *the exploration of color is her greatest pleasure when quiltmaking. Rebecca thinks of quilts as the conscious and unconscious expressions of our experiences with color. She never has an idea in mind before she begins a project. In* Sunny and Hazy, *the large light triangles, left-over from another project, sparked Rebecca's initial inspiration. By adding other triangles in yellow, she gave the quilt a particular atmospheric quality of light where familiar perceptions are altered. When designing a quilt, many of Rebecca's waking hours are spent sorting a wide variety of prints. This willingness for experimentation and her risk-taking with fabric and color, while using traditional, simple geometric patterns, are what shape her style. All of Rebecca's quilts express vigor and vitality.*

Sunny and Hazy
by Rebecca Rohrkaste

Traditional block pattern: Zigzag

FINISHED SIZE	82″ x 82″
VERTICAL ROWS: TOTAL	10
TRIANGLES PER ROW: TOTAL	12

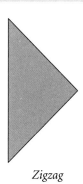

Zigzag

Yardage

Triangles and pieced borders:

    fabrics to total…**6¾ or eighteen ⅜ yard pieces**

Backing…**4¾**

Binding: ¼″ wide, finished…**½**

Cutting

Triangles

(A) 10⅜″ squares…**60** *Cut squares in **half diagonally.***

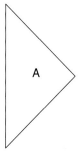

9½″ triangle

Border, Backing, and Binding

Side borders: width…**4″** *Cut strips of various lengths.*

Backing: lengths…**2**

    See piecing diagram (page 116) **A**

Binding: width…**1⅞″**

Construction

1. Sew ten triangles together to make ten vertical rows, as shown.
   ◆ *Helpful hint:* A design wall will be helpful for arranging the triangles in this quilt.
2. Sew a triangle to the top of one row, as shown.

Step 1   *Step 2*

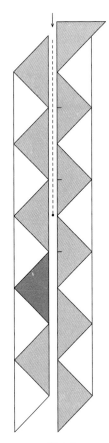

Step 3

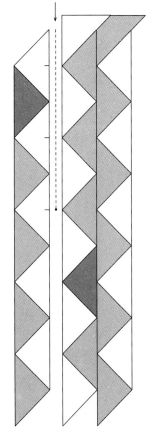

Step 5

3. Sew two rows of triangles together, stitching only halfway as indicated by the arrow and dot.
   ✦ *Helpful hint:* Pin first, matching the points of the triangles on one row to the centers of the triangles on the adjoining row.

4. Stitch a triangle to the top of the next row, as shown. Note that this triangle overlaps the end triangle of the previous row. Trim excess, as needed.

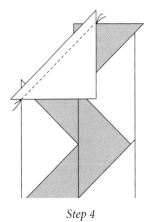

Step 4

5. Attach a third row of triangles in the same manner, stitching halfway and matching triangle points to adjoining triangle centers.

6. Continue joining rows, alternately adding a triangle and then attaching a row, stitching only halfway. End with a triangle stitched to the top of the tenth row of triangles.

7. Sew a triangle to the bottom of the tenth row. Stitch Rows 9 and 10 together to the previous stitching line. Alternately add a triangle and stitch the rows together, ending with a triangle on Row 1.

8. Sew a variety of random lengths of 4″-wide strips together for the pieced side borders. Note that there are two pieced borders per side.

9. Attach the pieced side borders to complete the quilt top.

Row 10   Row 9

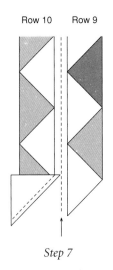

Step 7

On Their Wedding Day

THIS WEDDING QUILT was lovingly made for Kellie and Santiago in celebration of their special wedding day. The gift of a wedding quilt symbolizes a gift of happiness, one that honors the centuries old tradition of creating a soothing sanctuary by forming a perfect boudoir. The quilt pattern, Steps to the Altar, gives the perfect measure of merriment to this beautiful quilt. Wrapped in lovely paper, the wedding quilt offers a message of love's language: words of love stitched within the layers of off-white cottons.

On Their Wedding Day

by the authors

Traditonal block pattern: Steps to the Altar; machine quilted by Kathy Sandbach

ON THEIR WEDDING DAY

FINISHED SIZE	60½″ x 60½″
BLOCKS SET	6 x 6
STEPS TO THE ALTAR BLOCKS: TOTAL	36

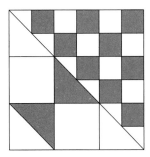

Steps to the Altar block

Yardage

Light colors: fabrics to total…**3**

Medium colors: fabrics to total…**2**

Backing…**3⅝**

Binding: ¼″ wide, finished…**½**

Cutting

Blocks

Light colors:

    (A) 2″-wide strips…**18**

    (B) 3½″-wide strips…**6** *Cut strips into 3½″ squares—need 72.*

    (C) 2⅜″-wide strips…**7** *Cut strips into 2⅜″ squares—need 108.*
        *Then cut the C squares in **half diagonally**.*

    (D) 3⅞″-wide strips…**6** *Cut strips into 3⅞″ squares—need 54.*
        *Then cut the D squares in **half diagonally**.*

Medium colors:

    (A) 2″-wide strips…**24** *Cut six strips into 2″ squares —need 108.*

    (D) 3⅞″-wide strips…**4** *Cut strips into 3⅞″ squares—need 36.*
        *Then cut the D squares in **half diagonally**.*

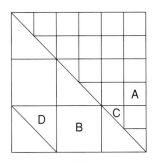

9″ block

Backing and Binding

Backing: lengths…**2**
    See piecing diagram (page 116) **A**

Binding: width…**1⅞″**

Construction

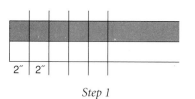

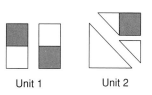

Step 1

1. Use the light and medium-colored strips to make eighteen sets. Then cut the sets apart every 2″, as shown.
2. Make units, as shown. Then check for accuracy. Each unit should measure 3½″. Refer to Part 2 (page 108) for help, if needed.
3. Block sew order: see diagram.
4. Arrange the blocks. Then sew the blocks together in a straight set, as shown.
5. Use the remaining Unit 1s from Step 2 for the pieced borders. Join 18 units for the top and bottom borders and 20 units for each side border. Attach the pieced borders to complete the quilt top.

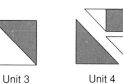

Unit 1   Unit 2

Unit 3   Unit 4

Step 2

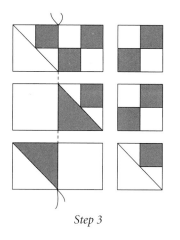

Step 3

Steps 4–5

Kathy Sandbach used the trapunto techniques in Hari Walner's book *Trapunto by Machine* (C&T Publishing) to enhance the quilt. We as authors recommend this book.

Grandmother's Choice

TWO FRIENDS…a shared passion…one dream. Diana McClun and Gayle Wells opened their fabric shop in 1980, knowing they would keep their shop stocked with beautiful fabrics for making quilts. Although they closed the retail business years later, they found a stack of blocks in the pattern, Grand-mother's Choice, from their first year of business. In 1996, Diana set the blocks together with vivid sash-ings…bringing pure delight and pleasure for two friends, one business, once again emerging with new life and memories.

Grandmother's Choice
by the authors

Traditional block pattern: Grandmother's Choice; quilted by Anna Venti

GRANDMOTHER'S CHOICE

FINISHED SIZE	67″ x 80″
BLOCKS SET	10 x 12
GRANDMOTHER'S CHOICE BLOCKS: TOTAL	120

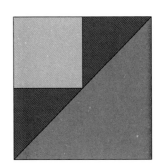

Grandmother's Choice block

Yardage

Grandmother's Choice blocks: fabrics to total…**3**

Short sashing strips: striped fabric for outer rows…**¾**
   and three additional fabrics, *each*…**½**

Long vertical sashing strips: three fabrics, *each*…**⅜**

Posts: fabrics to total…**⅜**

Border:
   Crosswise…**⅝**
   or lengthwise…**2 ¼**

Backing…**4 ¾**

Binding: ¼″ wide, finished…**⅝**

Cutting

Blocks

(A) 2 ¾″-wide strips…**8** *Cut strips into 2 ¾″ squares—need 120.*

(B) 3 ⅛″-wide strips…**10** *Cut strips into 3 ⅛″ squares—need 120.*
   Then cut the B squares in **half diagonally.**

(C) 5 ⅜″-wide strips…**9** *Cut strips into 5 ⅜″ squares—need 60.*
   Then cut the C squares in **half diagonally.**

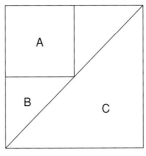

4 ½″ block

Sashing and Posts

Sashing strips (vertical and horizontal): width…**2½″**

Posts: 2½″ squares…**55**

Border, Backing, and Binding

Border: width…**2¼″**

Backing: lengths…**2**

    See piecing diagram (page 116) **A**

Binding: width…**1⅞″**

Construction

Step 1

1. Block sew order: see diagram.
2. Join the pieced blocks, short sashing strips, and posts into five vertical rows, as shown.
3. Sew five rows together, joining the rows with the long vertical sashing strips.

    ♦ *Helpful hint:* Use the average measurement of the vertical rows to determine the length of the sashing strips.
4. Attach the borders to complete the quilt top.

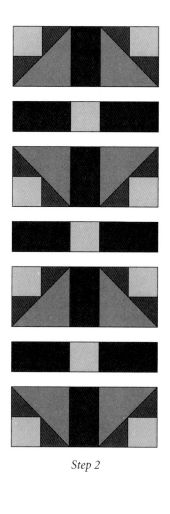

Step 2

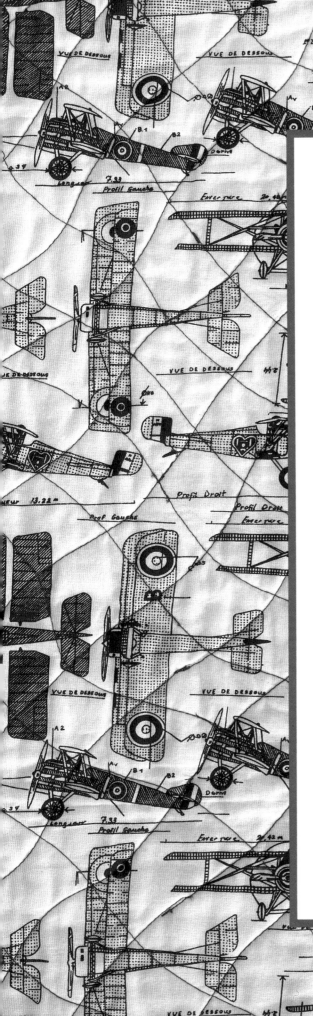

Airplanes for Big Brother

DIANA'S STORY

A part of living in the country, with the long snowy winters and without a television, meant that our family turned to hobbies for entertainment. I remember watching my brother making model airplanes, night after night, as the smell of glue and paint surrounded me. He would glue together millions of tiny balsa pieces to make his intricate models. While I made this quilt, I was tied to times and traditions gone by. The quilt tells of my brother growing up and his years of working for Boeing and the airplane industry. It also reminds me of my travels—each little plane representing a different teaching assignment to distant lands—where I would purchase and collect fabrics. The positive and negative spaces formed by the quilt's design illustrate the ups and downs of life's journey. But most of all, the quilt is a tribute to my big brother, who loved me in spite of my pesky self, and who loved our family…and the sense of adventure that only an airplane can bring. And so, Merry Christmas, to Don Hampton, my big brother.

Airplanes for Big Brother

by the authors

Traditional block pattern: Airplane; machine quilted by Kathy Sandbach

AIRPLANES FOR BIG BROTHER

FINISHED SIZE	80½″ x 80½″
BLOCKS SET	8 x 8
AIRPLANE BLOCKS: TOTAL	64

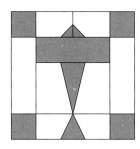

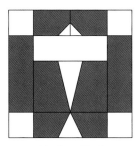

Airplane blocks

Yardage

Light colors: sixteen, *each*…**¼**

Dark colors: sixteen, *each*…**¼**

Backing…**5**

Binding: ¼″ wide, finished…**⅝**

Cutting

The template patterns E to H for *Airplanes for Big Brother* are on page 139.

Blocks

From *each* ¼ yard piece, cut the pieces as shown in the cutting diagram:

   (A) eight 2½″ squares

   (B) six 2½″ x 6½″ rectangles

   (C) four 2½″ x 3½″ rectangles

   (D) four 1½″ squares

   (E) two and two reversed with template

   (F) two with template

   (G) two and two reversed with template

   (H) two with template

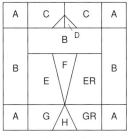

10″ block

Backing and Binding

Backing: lengths…**2**

   See piecing diagram (page 116) **A**

Binding: width…**1⅞″**

R= reverse template on fabric

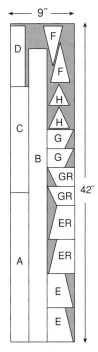

Cutting diagram

Construction

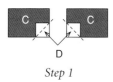

Step 1

Step 2

Note: Since this is a positive/negative setting, make 32 blocks using light backgrounds and 32 blocks using dark backgrounds.

1. Use the double half-square triangle technique to make the units, as shown. Refer to Part 2 (page 108) for help, if needed.
2. Unit construction: see diagram.
3. Block sew order: see diagrams.
4. Lay out all the blocks, alternating the light and dark blocks and reversing the direction, as shown in the photograph. Then sew the blocks together in a straight set (page 111).

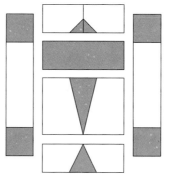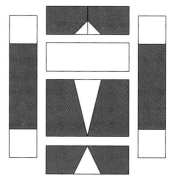

Step 3

Falling Leaves II

WHENEVER WE SEE a bright patchwork of glorious leaves, it reminds us of the bedding gardens at Freddy Moran's home. Each spring Freddy faithfully plants her garden so by summer it shows a carpet of gleaming colors. Freddy's extraordinary garden coaxes her outside every morning. These morning excursions provide her with a wonderland of ideas and endless inspiration. Freddy's quilts often reflect the many images she finds in her garden. Yet, this particular quilt didn't go together easily. Three different times Freddy had to work: she ripped out some blocks and rejected two or three borders. The lesson learned is that some quilts are indeed a struggle. Yet, with Freddy's persistence, Falling Leaves II survived, pleasing its maker with all its glory.

Falling Leaves II
by Freddy Moran

Traditional block pattern: Maple Leaf; machine quilted by Kathy Sandbach

FALLING LEAVES II

FINISHED SIZE	89″ x 89″
BLOCKS SET	6 x 6
MAPLE LEAF BLOCKS	
3″ BLOCKS: TOTAL	48
6″ BLOCKS: TOTAL	108
12″ BLOCKS: TOTAL	6

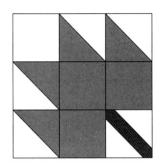

Maple Leaf block

Yardage

Backgrounds: fabrics to total…**3½**

Leaves and pieced border: fabrics to total…**5**

Stems: fabrics to total…**½**

Sashing and inner border:

    Crosswise…**1**

    or lengthwise…**2½**

Pieced border and outer border fabric:

    Crosswise…**1¾**

    or lengthwise…**2⅝**

Backing…**8**

Binding: ¼″ wide, finished…**⅝**

Cutting

Blocks

3″ blocks:

    Backgrounds:

        (A) 1½″-wide strips…**4** *Cut strips into 1½″ squares—need 96.*

        (B) 1⅞″-wide strips…**5** *Cut strips into 1⅞″ squares—need 96.*

        *Then cut the B squares in **half diagonally.***

    Leaves:

        (A) 1½″ squares…**3 per block**

        (B) 1⅞″ squares…**2 per block** *Cut the B squares in **half diagonally.***

6″ blocks:

    Backgrounds:

        (C) 2½″-wide strips…**7** *Cut strips into 2½″ squares—need 108.*

        (D) 2⅞″-wide strips…**16** *Cut strips into 2⅞″ squares—need 216.*

        *Then cut the D squares in **half diagonally.***

        (F) 2½″-wide strips…**7** *Cut strips into 2½″ squares—need 108.*

        *Then cut the F squares in **half diagonally.***

3″ block

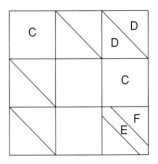

6″ block

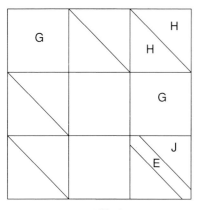

12″ block

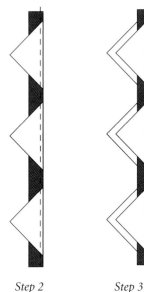

Step 2   *Step 3*

Step 4

Leaves:

(C) 2½″ squares…**3 per block**

(D) 2⅞″ squares…**2 per block**

*Cut the D squares in **half diagonally**.*

12″ blocks:

Backgrounds:

(G) 4½″-wide strip…**1** *Cut strip into 4½″ squares—need 6.*

(H) 4⅞″-wide strips…**2** *Cut strips into 4⅞″ squares—need 12.*
*Then cut the H squares in **half diagonally**.*

(J) 4½″-wide strip…**1** *Cut strip into 4½″ squares—need 6.*
*Then cut the J squares in **half diagonally**.*

Leaves:

(G) 4½″ squares…**3 per block**

(H) 4⅞″ squares…**2 per block**

*Cut the H squares in **half diagonally**.*

Stems (6″ and 12″ blocks):

(E) 1″-wide strips…**11**

Sashing, Borders, Backing, and Binding

Sashing and inner border: width…**1″**

Pieced border:

2⅞″-wide strips (use leaves fabrics)…**12** *Cut strips into 2⅞″ squares—need 168. Then cut the squares in **half diagonally**.*

2½″-wide strips (use outer border fabric*)…**11**
Cut strips into 2½″ squares—need 168.

Outer border: width…**3″**

*Cut the outer border strips first if making lengthwise cuts.

Backing: lengths…**3**

See piecing diagram (page 116) **C**

Binding: width…**1⅞″**

Construction

1. Make the half-square triangle units for all the blocks, referring to Part 2 (page 107) for help if needed.

2. Make the stem units for the 6″ and 12″ blocks. Sew F and J pieces to the E stem strips, with right sides together, as shown. Then press the seams toward the stem strips.

3. Sew F and J pieces to the opposite side of the stem strip, matching the triangles, as shown. Press the seams toward the stem strips.

4. Cut the stem units, as shown.

5. Block sew order: see diagrams.

6. Arrange the blocks, as shown in the photograph. Then sew the blocks together in a straight set (page 112) with the narrow sashing strips.

   ◆ *Helpful hint:* Use the average measurement of the blocks and rows to determine the length of the sashing strips.

7. From the leaves fabric, make the half-square triangle units for the pieced border. Then sew the units to the 2½″ squares of outer border fabric, as shown.

8. Sew a narrow inner border and a pieced border to opposite sides of the quilt top.

9. Sew a narrow inner border to the top and bottom.

10. Sew a short sashing strip to each end of the top and bottom pieced borders. Then sew a corner unit to each end of the borders.

11. Attach the outer borders to complete the quilt top.

Step 7

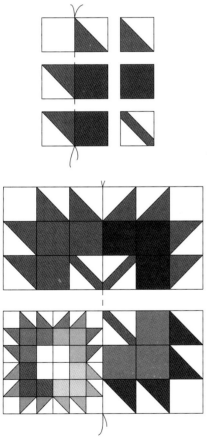

Step 5

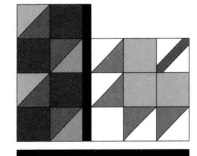
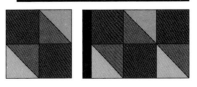

Steps 8–10

Hearts

THE SIMPLICITY of the heart motif holds special meaning: it reminds us of people who have touched our lives. When Diana was a child, the heart motif was deeply embedded in her life. Diana recalls pleasant times spent cutting volumes of paper hearts. Rows of folded valentines lined her windows as a child. Years later, customers came into her shop requesting paper heart patterns. Why is a heart so common and simple, so liked and honored? Hearts send wishes of love, happiness, and good health. When we look deep in our hearts, we discover love. This feeling permeates our lives. And a quilted heart is a soft heart. In each book we've written, a space has been devoted for a heart quilt. This book is no exception!

by the authors

Original Heart block pattern by the authors; machine quilted by Kathy Sandbach

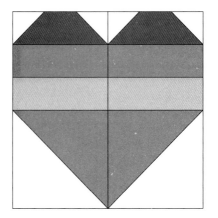

Large Heart block

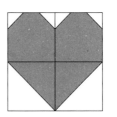

Medium and Small Heart blocks

FINISHED SIZE	62″ x 73½″
SMALL HEARTS: TOTAL	62
MEDIUM HEARTS: TOTAL	14
LARGE HEARTS: TOTAL	14

Yardage

Backgrounds: fabrics to total...**2**
Hearts: fabrics to total...**3½**
Sashings: fabrics to total...**¼**
Backing...**3¾**
Binding: ¼″ wide, finished...**½**

Cutting

Blocks

Small Heart blocks:

    Backgrounds:

        (G) 1″-wide strips...**6** *Cut strips into 1″ squares—need 248.*

        (I) 3⅛″-wide strips...**5** *Cut strips into 3⅛″ squares—need 62.*
           *Then cut the I squares in **half diagonally.***

    Hearts:

        (H) 2¾″-wide strips...**7**
           Cut strips into 2¼″ x 2¾″ rectangles—need 124.

        (I) 3⅛″-wide strips...**5** *Cut strips into 3⅛″ squares—need 62.*
           *Then cut the I squares in **half diagonally.***

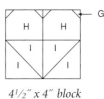

4½″ x 4″ block

Medium Heart blocks:

    Backgrounds:

        (D) 1½″-wide strips...**2** *Cut the strips into 1½″ squares—need 56.*

        (F) 3⅞″-wide strips...**2** *Cut the strips into 3⅞″ squares—need 14.*
           *Then cut the F squares in **half diagonally.***

    Hearts:

        (E) 3½″-wide strips...**3** *Cut strips into 3½″ squares—need 28.*

        (F) 3⅞″-wide strips...**2** *Cut strips into 3⅞″ squares—need 14.*
           *Then cut the F squares in **half diagonally.***

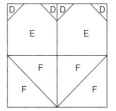

6″ block

Large Heart blocks:

    Backgrounds:

        (A) $2\frac{1}{2}''$-wide strips…**4** *Cut the strips into $2\frac{1}{2}''$ squares—need 56.*

        (C) $6\frac{7}{8}''$ squares…**14** *Cut the squares in **half diagonally**.*

    Hearts:

        (B) $2\frac{1}{2}''$ x $6\frac{1}{2}''$ pieces…**6 per block**

        (C) $6\frac{7}{8}''$ squares…**14** *Cut the squares in **half diagonally**.*

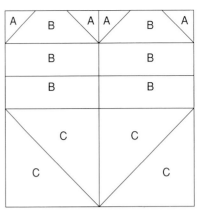

12″ block

Sashings, Backing, and Binding

Sashing: widths (refer to the diagram on page 38 for placement)

    (1)…**$1\frac{1}{4}''$**

    (2)…**$1\frac{1}{2}''$**

    (3)…**$2\frac{1}{4}''$**

    (4)…**$2\frac{1}{2}''$**

    (5)…**$3\frac{1}{4}''$**

    (6)…**$3\frac{1}{2}''$**

    (7)…**$3\frac{3}{4}''$**

Backing: lengths…**2**

    See piecing diagram (page 116) **B**

Binding: width…**$1\frac{7}{8}''$**

Construction

1. Use the double half-square triangle technique to make units, as shown. When making the large hearts, sew together three $2\frac{1}{2}''$ x $6\frac{1}{2}''$ pieces as units before attaching the corners, as shown.

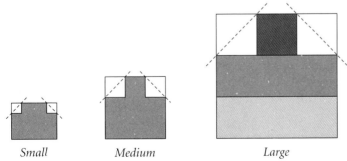

Small   *Medium*   *Large*

Step 1

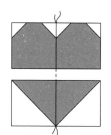

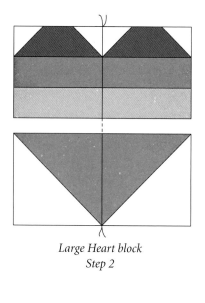

Medium and Small Heart blocks
Step 2

2. Make half-square triangles for all sizes. Then sew the units together to complete the blocks, as shown. Note some of the smaller hearts use two fabrics for variety.

3. Sew the blocks together in sections. Then join the sections with the pieced sashing strips, referring to the diagram for help with placement.

◆ *Helpful hint:* Use measurement of the row(s) to determine length of sashing strips.

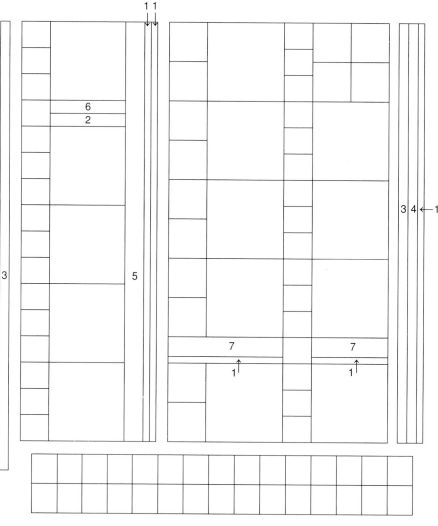

Large Heart block
Step 2

Step 3

Molly's Magic Pansies

LAURA'S STORY

*Fresh as a flower, full of life and love…
that's my Molly Rose! Molly calls her
quilt her "magic blanket." In our family, a magic blanket is a quilt that is
stitched with love. If anyone is in need
of attention, the quilt is freely shared.
Only a magic blanket has the special
power to heal: it can make even the
worst tummy ache feel better. Because
the magic of the pansy also generates
special excitement, we chose Diana's
Pansy block, which inspired us to use
all the vibrant colors so reflective of
Molly's lively personality. If loving
stitches make magical quilts, this one
is exceptional!*

Molly's Magic Pansies
by the authors

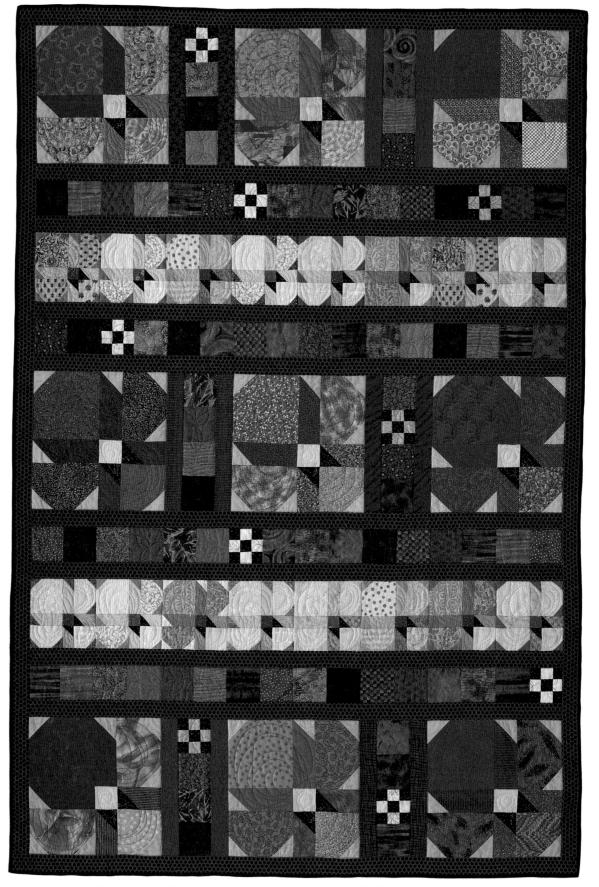

Original Pansy block pattern by the authors; machine quilted by Kathy Sandbach

FINISHED SIZE	51½″ x 75½″
PANSY BLOCKS	
6″ BLOCKS: TOTAL	16
12″ BLOCKS: TOTAL	9

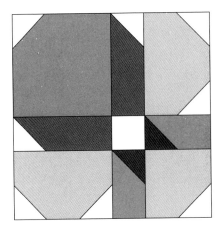

Pansy block

Yardage

Backgrounds: fabrics to total…**1**

Pansies: fabrics to total…**2 ⅝**

Centers: fabrics to total…**⅝**

Pieced sashing units: fabrics to total…**1**

    Nine-Patches: two fabrics, *each*…**¼**

Vertical sashing strips: fabrics to total…**⅜**

Horizontal sashing strips and border:

    Crosswise…**1**

    or lengthwise…**2 ⅛**

Backing…**3 ¼**

Binding: ¼″ wide, finished…**½**

3″ Nine-Patch block

Cutting

Blocks

6″ blocks:

  Backgrounds:

    (G) 1½″-wide strips…**5**

    Cut strips into 1½″ squares—need 128.

  Pansies:

    (B) 2½″ square…**1 per block**

    (C) 2½″ x 3½″ pieces…**2 per block**

    (D) 3½″ square…**1 per block**

    (E) 1½″ x 2½″ pieces…**2 per block**

    (F) 1½″ x 3½″ pieces…**2 per block**

  Centers:

    (A) 1½″-wide strip…**1** *Cut strip into 1½″ squares—need 16.*

    (H) 1½″-wide strips…**2** *Cut strips into 1½″ squares—need 32.*

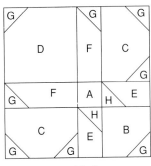

6″ block

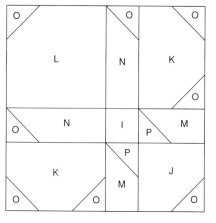

12″ block

12″ blocks:

Background:

(O) 2½″-wide strips…**5**

Cut strips into 2½″ squares—need 72.

Pansies:

(J) 4½″ square…**1 per block**

(K) 4½″ x 6½″ pieces…**2 per block**

(L) 6½″ square…**1 per block**

(M) 2½″ x 4½″ pieces…**2 per block**

(N) 2½″ x 6½″ pieces…**2 per block**

Centers:

(I) 2½″-wide strip…**1** *Cut strip into 2½″ squares—need 9.*

(P) 2½″-wide strips…**2** *Cut strips into 2½″ squares—need 18.*

Sashings, Borders, Backing, and Binding

Pieced sashing units: 3½″ squares…**79**

Nine-Patches: 1½″-wide strips, *each* of two fabrics…**3**

Vertical sashing strips: 2″ x 12½″ pieces…**12**

Horizontal sashing strips and border: width…**2″**

Backing: lengths…**2**

See piecing diagram (page 116) **B**

Binding: width…**1⅞″**

Construction

1. Use the double half-square triangle technique in Part 2 (page 108) to attach the G and O squares of background fabric to make the units, as shown.

6" block

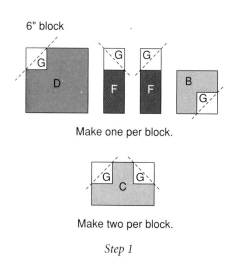

Make one per block.

Make two per block.

Step 1

12" block

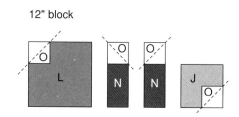

Make one per block.

Make two per block.

Step 1

2. Use the double half-square triangle technique in Part 2 (page 108) to attach the H and P squares of fabric to make the units, as shown.

3. Block sew order: see diagram.

4. Make the Nine-Patch blocks, as shown.

5. Make six vertical sashing units, as shown. Then make four horizontal sashing units.

   ♦ *Helpful hint:* Refer to the diagram for the exact placement of the Nine-Patch blocks.

6. Sew all the blocks and sashing units together, as shown.

7. Attach the border strips to complete the quilt top.

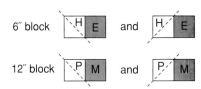

Step 2

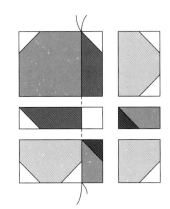

Step 3

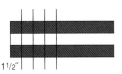

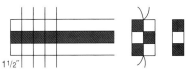

Step 4

Vertical sashing units

Horizontal sashing units

Step 5

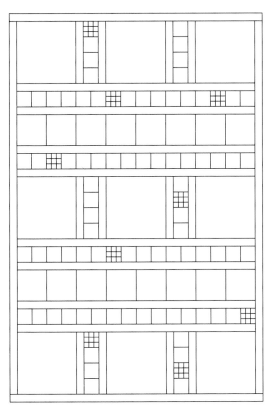

Steps 6–7

Where's William?

When Laura first met and fell in love with her husband Bill, he wore exclusively plaid flannel shirts. Of course, when she thought of fabrics to make this quilt, it was certainly appropriate he should have a plaid flannel quilt. Bill truly appreciates the pristine beauty of the great outdoors, and it has become his quiet refuge. Often you can see him hiking among the pine trees. So in order that he be comfortable on the trail, Laura chose a Tree pattern. Also, she hid some pictures of Bill among the trees, since he often jokes that there has yet to be a picture of him in any of the books. If you ever meet Bill on a trail, please mention to him that you have found William Nownes in this book.

Where's William?
by the authors

Original Tree block pattern by the authors

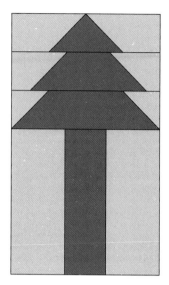

Tree block

FINISHED SIZE	79½″ x 78″
TREE BLOCKS	
6″ BLOCKS: TOTAL	48
9″ BLOCKS: TOTAL	16
12″ BLOCKS: TOTAL	18

Yardage

Background…**4½**

Trees and inner border: fabrics to total…**4½**

Trunks: fabrics to total…**½**

Sashing, and binding: ½″ wide, finished
  Crosswise…**1½**
  or lengthwise…**2**

Backing…**4¾**

Cutting

Blocks

6″ blocks:

  Background: 2″-wide strips…**27**

    Then cut strips as follows:

    (D) eight strips into 2″ x 3½″ rectangles—need 96.

    (E) seven strips into 2″ x 2¾″ rectangles—need 96.

    (F) five strips into 2″ squares—need 96.

    (G) seven strips into 2″ x 3″ rectangles—need 96.

  Trees: 2″-wide strips…**24** *(Note: each 2″-wide strip makes two trees.)*

    Then cut *each* strip into the following pieces:

    (A) two 2″ x 3½″ rectangles.

    (B) two 2″ x 5″ rectangles.

    (C) two 2″ x 6½″ rectangles.

  Trunks: (H) 1½″ x 2″ pieces…**48**

6″ block

9″ blocks:

    Background: 2¾″-wide strips…**11**

        Then cut strips as follows:

            (L) four strips into 2¾″ x 5″ rectangles—need 32.

            (M) four strips into 2¾″ x 3⅞″ rectangles—need 32.

            (N) three strips into 2¾″ squares—need 32.

    (O) 3¾″-wide strip…**1**

        Cut strip into 3¾″ x 9″ rectangles—need 4.

    Trees: 2¼″-wide strips…**8** *(Note: each 2¼″-wide strip makes two trees)*

        Then cut *each* strip into the following pieces:

            (I) two 2¾″ x 5″ rectangles.

            (J) two 2¾″ x 7¼″ rectangles.

            (K) two 2¾″ x 9½″ rectangles.

    Trunks: (P) 3″ x 9″ pieces…**2**

12″ blocks:

    Background: 3½″-wide strips…**14**

        Then cut strips as follows:

            (T) six strips into 3½″ x 6½″ rectangles (need 36).

            (U) five strips into 3½″ x 5″ rectangles (need 36).

            (V) three strips into 3½″ squares (need 36).

    (W) 5″-wide strips…**2**

        Cut strips into 5″ x 9″ rectangles—need 6.

    Trees: 3½″-wide strips…**18** *(Note: each 3½″-wide strip makes one tree.)*

        Then cut *each* strip into the following pieces:

            (Q) one 3½″ x 6½″ rectangle.

            (R) one 3½″ x 9½″ rectangle.

            (S) one 3½″ x 12½″ rectangle.

    Trunks: (X) 3½″ x 9″ pieces…**3**

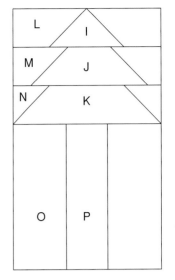

9″ block

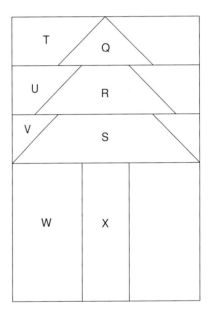

12″ block

Sashing, Border, Backing, and Binding

Sashing: width…**3″**

Pieced border: 2″-wide strips…**21** *(vary lengths from 11″ to 18″)*

Backing: lengths…**2**

    See piecing diagram (page 116) **A**

Binding: width…**2¾″**

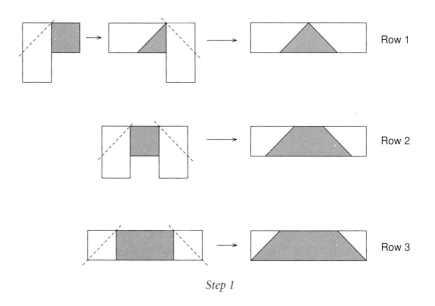

Step 1

Construction

1. Unit construction: see diagrams. Use the double half-square triangle technique to make the units, as shown. Refer to Part 2 (page 108) for help, if needed.

   ✦ *Helpful hint:* To reduce any waste, make bonus half-square triangles which can be used for another project. To do so, add another stitching line, as shown. Then cut between the stitching lines. Press to make the half-square triangle, as shown.

2. Block sew order: see diagram. Note only two 9″ blocks and three 12″ blocks have the trunk sections.

3. Arrange all the 9″ and 12″ trees, as shown in the photograph. Sew the blocks together in vertical rows. Then join the rows together with sashing strips.

   ✦ *Helpful hint:* Use the average measurement of the rows to determine the length of the sashing strips.

4. Sew several short border strips together for the needed length of each side of the quilt top. Attach the strips to all sides of the quilt top, trimming the excess border lengths, as needed.

5. Make the pieced borders using the 6″ blocks. Join 13 blocks for the top and bottom borders and 11 blocks for each side border. Attach the pieced side borders, and then the top and bottom borders to complete the quilt top.

6. The quilt is tied with wool yarn, using square knots. An additional layer of batting is used.

   ✦ *Helpful hint:* Leave a ¼″ extension of batting and backing to fill the wider binding.

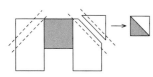

Bonus half-square triangles

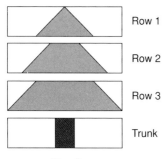

Step 2

Peggy's Baskets

BERNICE McCOY STONE *felt privileged to have Peggy Kitchen as a dear quilting friend. And it was through a quilt that these two friends formed one of their most enduring bonds. Their shared excitement over an antique quilt that Peggy had purchased for $25.00 led Bernice to re-create the quilt, applying her personal interpretation. Since Bernice is a traditionalist who honors and admires the quiltmaker of past times, she kept the original small basket design, changing only the color and setting. When Peggy passed away in 1994, her son, John, brought the antique quilt to Bernice as a gift to honor the friendship and the memory of his mother, Peggy Kitchen.*

Peggy's Baskets
by Bernice McCoy Stone

Traditional block pattern: Basket; quilted by Rebecca Coleman Rouch

PEGGY'S BASKETS

FINISHED SIZE	87" x 98"
BLOCKS SET	11 x 13
BASKET BLOCKS: TOTAL	143
ALTERNATE BLOCKS: TOTAL	120
PIECED BORDER UNITS: TOTAL	228

Basket block

Yardage

Background (includes pieced border)…**3⅝**

Baskets: fabrics to total…**2¼**

Alternate blocks, side and corner triangles, and borders…**5½**

Pieced border (dark triangles)…**1⅜**

Backing…**7¾**

Binding (bias): ¼" wide, finished…**1¼**

Pieced border unit

Cutting

The template pattern E for *Peggy's Baskets* is on page 139.

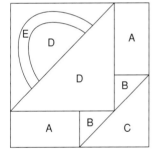

4" block

Basket Blocks

Background:

    (A) 2½"-wide strips…**11**

        Cut strips into 1½" x 2½" rectangles—need 286.

    (C) 2⅞"-wide strips…**6** *Cut strips into 2⅞" squares—need 72.*

        *Then cut the squares in **half diagonally.***

    (D) 3⅞"-wide strips…**8** *Cut strips into 3⅞" squares—need 72.*

        *Then cut the squares in **half diagonally.***

Baskets:

    (B) 1⅞"-wide strips…**4** *Cut strips into 1⅞" squares—need 143.*

        *Then cut the squares in **half diagonally.***

    (D) 3⅞"-wide strips…**15** *Cut strips into 3⅞" squares—need 143.*

        *Then cut the squares in **half diagonally**. One half will be used for the handles.*

Handles: use one half of the D triangles (above) with template E.

Alternate Blocks, Side and Corner Triangles, and Borders

Alternate blocks:

4½″-wide strips...**14** *Cut strips into 4½″ squares—need 120.*

Side triangles:

7″-wide strips...**2** *Cut strips into 7″ squares—need 11.*

*Then cut the squares into **quarters diagonally.***

Corner triangles:

4¼″ squares...**2** *Cut squares in **half diagonally.***

Inner border: width...**7¾″**

Outer border: width...**2¾″**

Pieced Border

Background:

(F) 2″-wide strips...**22** *Cut strips into 2″ squares—need 456.*

Dark triangles:

(G) 3½″-wide strips...**11** *Cut strips into 2″ x 3½″ rectangles—need 228.*

Backing and Binding

Backing: lengths...**3**

See piecing diagram (page 116) **D**

Binding: width, cut on bias...**1⅞″**

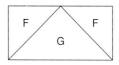

1½″ x 3″ unit

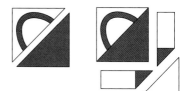

Step 2

Step 3

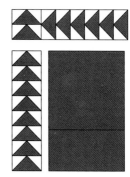

Step 6

Construction

1. Use the needle-turn method of appliqué in Part 2 (page 110) to sew the basket handles to the background triangles.
2. Block sew order: see diagrams.
3. Use the double half-square triangle technique to make the units for the pieced border, as shown. Refer to Part 2 (page 108) for help, if needed.
4. Sew the pieced blocks, alternate blocks, and side and corner triangles together in a diagonal set (page 113). The side and corner triangles are cut slightly too large to allow for straightening the quilt edges. Trim the excess fabric to within ⅜″ of the corners of the blocks.
5. Attach the inner borders.
6. Make the pieced borders using the double half-square triangle units. Use 55 units for the top and bottom borders, and 59 units for each side border. Note the direction of the corner units in the top and bottom borders, as shown.
7. Attach the pieced borders. Then attach the outer borders to complete the quilt top.

Cups & Saucers

DIANA'S STORY

Who doesn't love a party? All my life I have been drawn to parties…yet, the day my daughters and friends gathered together for an old-fashioned tea party to celebrate my birthday, I was so surprised. Normally, I am never, ever surprised, but this day I had another agenda, and the thought of a party had never occurred to me. For days, my daughters Katie Prindle and Tricia Thomas, my daughter-in-law Erin McClun, my niece Karen McArdle, and my co-author Laura Nownes had worked at making preparations for this extraordinary event. The party was exclusively for women: silver trays, starched white linens, and a house full of flowers provided the perfect ambiance. To make the quilt, my friends had secretly taken all the fabrics, along with the border fabric, from my home—right under my nose! They knew where to find my collection of Liberty® of London fabrics from my travels to England and they even knew of my secret stash of Liberties. Each cup and saucer was pieced with a different fabric and carefully appliquéd with the finest of stitches. This quilt holds all the memories of a fun-filled party where I was surrounded by a room full of loved friends and my gorgeous family. Thank you, wonderful women!

Cups & Saucers

by Katie Prindle, Tricia Thomas, Erin McClun, Karen McArdle, and Laura Nownes

Traditional block pattern: Cup and Saucer; quilted by Anna Venti

Cup and Saucer block

CUPS & SAUCERS

FINISHED SIZE	90″ x 102″
BLOCKS SET	10 x 12
CUP AND SAUCER BLOCKS: TOTAL	120

Yardage

Background…**2⅝**

Cups and Saucers: fabrics to total…**2⅞**

Shelf:

Crosswise…**1**

or lengthwise…**1⅝**

Inner border:

Crosswise…**⅞**

or lengthwise…**2⅜**

Outer border:

12½″ wide border-print fabric…**12**

or 10″ wide border from 42″ wide fabric…**3**

Backing…**8**

Binding: ¼″ wide, finished…**¾**

Cutting

The template pattern E for *Cups & Saucers* is on page 139.

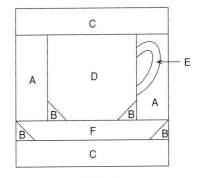

6″ block

Blocks

Background:

(A) 1¾″-wide strips…**22**

Cut strips into 1¾″ x 3¾″ rectangles—need 240.

(B) 1¼″-wide strips…**15** *Cut strips into 1¼″ squares—need 480.*

(C) 1¼″-wide strips…**20**

Cut strips into 1½″ x 6½″ rectangles—need 120.

Cup and Saucer:

(D) 3¾″ x 4″ pieces…**120**

(F) 1¼″ x 6½″ pieces…**120**

Handles: use template E…**120**

Shelf:

(C) 1½″-wide strips…**20*****

Cut strips into 1½″ x 6½″ rectangles—need 120.

✦ *Helpful hint:* To avoid unnecessary seams, cut the shelf fabric as horizontal sashing strips (approximately 62″ long) and sew the strips to the bottom of each row of blocks, as shown.

Helpful hint

Borders, Backing, and Binding

Inner border: width…**3¾″**

Outer border: width…**10″ or 12½″**

Backing: lengths…**3**

See piecing diagram (page 116) **D**

Binding: width…**1⅞″**

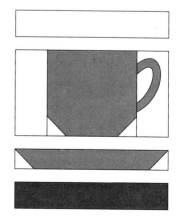

Step 1

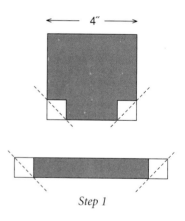

Step 3

Construction

1. Use the double half-square triangle technique in Part 2 (page 108) to make the units, as shown. ➤*Warning:* The cup is slightly wider than it is high. Check placement before stitching the corners.

2. Use the needle-turn method to appliqué the handles to the background piece. Refer to Part 2 (page 110) for help, if needed.

3. Block sew order: see diagram.

4. Sew the blocks together in a straight set. Refer to Part 2 (page 111) for help, if needed.

5. Join the inner and outer border strips in pairs lengthwise. Then attach them to the quilt top and miter the corners. Refer to Part 2 (page 114) for help, if needed.

Bunny-Go-Around

PART OF THE MYSTERY behind every quilt is imagining why the quilt was made. Yet, one of the most fulfilling reasons a quilter may have is often the simplest: I made this quilt for myself! When Kathy Levesque decided to create her own quilt, she knew she wanted a folk-art composition. Although many artists who work in this style add numerous motifs of all sizes going in all directions, Kathy chose a more symmetrical approach. She gave the red tulips an orderly presentation around the plump little birds. The circle of bunnies adds to the order a rhythm and balance that is contained within the border. Reflecting Kathy's design awareness, this quilt is a blend of spatial harmony and balance. The quilt is a very pleasing tribute to its maker.

Bunny-Go-Around
by Kathy Levesque

Original appliqué designs by Kathy Levesque; traditional block pattern: Log Cabin

BUNNY-GO-AROUND

FINISHED SIZE	48½″ x 48½″
LOG CABIN BLOCKS: TOTAL	36
PLAIN BLOCKS: TOTAL	64

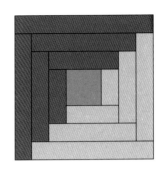

Log Cabin block

Yardage

Light colors (Plain and Log Cabin blocks): fabrics to total…**1¾**

Dark colors (Leaves, Outer border, and Log Cabin blocks): fabrics to total…**2**

Log Cabin centers, Hearts, Tulips, and Inner border: fabrics to total…**⅝**

Birds and Bunnies: fabrics to total…**½**

Backing…**3**

Binding: ¼″ wide, finished…**⅜**

Cutting

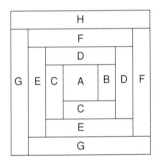

4″ block

The template patterns J to Q for *Bunny-Go-Around* are on page 143.

Blocks

Light colors:

    Plain blocks: 4½″ squares…**64**

    Log Cabin blocks: 1″-wide strips…**17**

        Then cut the strips into the following rectangles: thirty-six *each*

        (B) 1″ x 1½″

        (C) 1″ x 2″

        (D) 1″ x 2½″

        (E) 1″ x 3″

        (F) 1″ x 3½″

        (G) 1″ x 4″

Dark colors:

    Outer border:

        4″ squares…**4**

        4″ x 40½″ pieces…**4**

Log Cabin blocks: 1″-wide strips…**19**

Then cut the strips into the following rectangles: thirty-six *each*

(C) 1″ x 2″

(D) 1″ x 2½″

(E) 1″ x 3″

(F) 1″ x 3½″

(G) 1″ x 4″

(H) 1″ x 4½″

Leaves: use template N…**8**

Inner border:

1″ x 40″ pieces…**4**

1″ x 4″ pieces…**4**

1″ x 4½″ pieces…**4**

Log Cabin centers:

(A) 1½″-wide strips…**2** *Cut strips into 1½″ squares—need 36.*

Hearts:

Small: use template K…**2**

Medium: use template L…**1**

Large: use template M…**4**

Tulips: use template O…**8**

Birds: use templates P and Q…**2 and 2R* each**

Bunnies: use template J…**8**

Backing and Binding

Backing: lengths…**2**

See piecing diagram (page 116) **A**

Binding: width…**1⅞″**

*R= reverse template on fabric

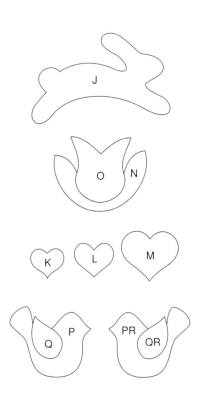

Construction

1. Construct 36 Log Cabin blocks, referring to the diagrams for sew order.

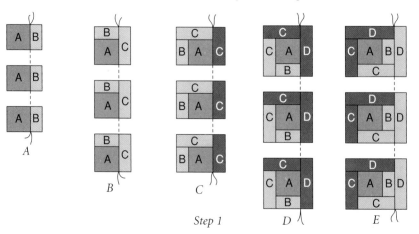

Step 1

2. Arrange all the pieced and plain blocks, referring to the photograph for help. Then sew them together in a straight set (page 111).

3. Prepare the appliquéd motifs, referring to Part 2 (page 109) for help, if needed. Appliqué the shapes in place, as shown in both the diagram and photograph.

4. Construct the corner blocks, as shown. Then join the inner and outer border strips in pairs.

5. Attach the borders and then corner blocks, as shown.

Step 4

Step 5

Grammy's Goose

INTO THE MIDST of Andrea and Ken Smith's lives enters a new life…a new baby…a new grandchild for their parents …and, a new quilt from Grammy Marna. Within the Eyring clan, tradition calls for each family to receive a hand-made quilt. The tradition started when the family of young Tanner, the first grandchild of Phil and Marna, received a Heart quilt from Grammy. Now little Talliya and her parents have become the happy recipients of Grammy's Goose quilt. Talliya's quilt was especially designed from the wallpaper and fabric her mom used to decorate her nursery. Grammy Marna and Diana McClun, friends forever, gathered together to make the quilt, spending happy moments designing, piecing, and, of course, chatting. A loving sentiment, this baby quilt celebrates the birth of a new baby into a beautiful new family and a peaceful world.

Grammy's Goose
by Marna Eyring

Original goose appliqué design by the authors; traditional block pattern: Baby Bunting

GRAMMY'S GOOSE

Baby Bunting block

Goose block

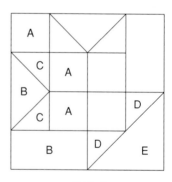

6″ block

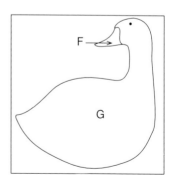

6″ block

FINISHED SIZE	45½″ x 45½″
BLOCKS SET	5 x 5
BABY BUNTING BLOCKS: TOTAL	12
GOOSE BLOCKS: TOTAL	13

Yardage

Light color: Baby Bunting background and Goose…**1**
Medium color: Goose background…**⅝**
Baby Bunting blocks, posts, corner blocks, and pieced border:
     fabrics to total…**1½**
Goose bill…**⅛**
Sashing…**⅝**
Backing…**2⅞**
Binding: ¼″ wide, finished…**½**

Cutting

The template patterns G and F for *Grammy's Goose* are on page 141.

Blocks, Posts, Corner Blocks, and Pieced Border

Light color:
Baby Bunting background:
   (A) 2″-wide strips…**2** *Cut strips into 2″ squares—need 36.*
   (B) 3½″-wide strips…**3** *Cut strips into 2″ x 3½″ rectangles—need 48.*
   (E) 3⅞″-wide strip…**1** *Cut strip into 3⅞″ squares—need 6.*
     *Then cut the E squares in **half diagonally**.*
Goose: use template G…**9 and 4R***

Medium color:
Goose background:
   6½″-wide strips…**3** *Cut strips into 6½″ squares—need 13.*

Baby Bunting blocks:
   (A) 2″ squares…**2 per block**
   (C) 2″ squares…**4 per block**
   (D) 2⅜″ squares…**1 per block** *Cut D squares in **half diagonally**.*

Posts:

2″-wide strips…**2** *Cut strips into 2″ squares—need 36.*

Pieced border:

2″-wide strips…**13**

Corner blocks:

3½″ squares…**4**

Goose bill: use template F…**9 and 4R***

Sashing:

2″-wide strips…**10** *Cut strips into 2″ x 6½″ rectangles—need 55.*

Backing: lengths…**2**

See piecing diagram (page 116) **A**

Binding: width…**1⅞″**

*R= reverse template on fabric

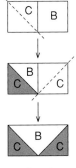

Step 1

Construction

1. Use the double half-square triangle technique to make the units, as shown.
2. Block sew order: see diagrams.
3. Appliqué a goose to each 6½″ square of medium-colored fabric. Reverse the direction for four of the geese. Use a permanent marking pen or embroider a French knot for the eye of each goose.
4. Join the pieced blocks and appliquéd blocks with the sashing and posts.
5. Cut the darkest strip of pieced border fabric into eight 2″ x 3½″ rectangles. Cut the remaining 2″-wide strips of border fabrics in half to make 22″ lengths. Randomly select strips and sew into four sets with six strips each. Then cut the sets apart every 3½″, as shown.
6. Borders: sew four 3½″ cut sets together. Then add a dark 2″ x 3½″ rectangle on opposite ends to bring it to the required length for the border strips.
7. Sew two pieced border strips to opposite sides of the quilt top.
8. Sew the corner blocks to opposite ends of the two remaining pieced border strips. Then attach these strips to complete the quilt top.

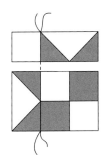

Step 2

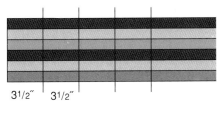

3½″   3½″

Step 5

Grandmother's Exotic Garden

TO HONOR THE MEMORY of her grand-parents, Linda Morand decided to create a quilt for the "Childhood Memories" Santa Rosa Quilt Guild Challenge. In order to satisfy the challenge rules, the quilt design needed to depict a scene from her childhood. Recalling the memories of her grandparents, Linda chose to convey her feelings for her grandmother and her wonderful garden full of exotic plants and flowers. Within the design, Linda formed a giant cross, a variation of the traditional Grandmother's Cross block, to illustrate her grandmother's strong religious faith and dedication to her church. At the point where the arms of the cross meet in the center is the Contrary Wife block, which reveals the assertive side of this strong-minded, midwestern woman. To convey her grandmother's playful, creative side—she was still very much a girl at heart even in her old age—oversize flowers, having outgrown their pots, dance around the center of the quilt with their leaves bowing and waving to the viewer. The big, red flowers are a reminder of the California poppies that her grandpa would plant around the grounds of their church. Every spring, the church lot shone with a blaze of color for Easter. This quilt captures both the color and character of two extraordinary people, Bill and Dorothy Broad Zulch.

Grandmother's Exotic Garden
by Linda Morand

Original Grandmother's Exotic Garden block pattern by Linda Morand

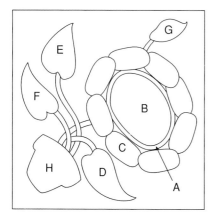

Grandmother's Exotic Garden
12″ block

FINISHED SIZE 37½″ x 37½″

EXOTIC BLOCKS: TOTAL 4

Yardage

Background: includes center unit…**¾**

Flower centers:

    template A…**¼**

    template B…**⅛**

Flower petals and bud: templates C and G…**¼**

Leaves: templates D, E, F…**⅛**

Stems…**½**

Flower pots: template H…**⅛**

Sashing

    Crosswise…**¼**

    or lengthwise…**⅜**

Center unit…**scraps**

Pieced borders:

    Background…**⅝**

    Inner border triangles…**⅛**

    Outer border triangles (includes center unit): two fabrics, *each*…**¼**

Backing…**1¼**

Binding: ¾″-wide, finished…**⅜**

Cutting

The template patterns A to H for *Grandmother's Exotic Garden* are on page 142.

Blocks

Exotic blocks:

    Background: 12½″ squares…**4**

    Flower centers:

        use template A…**4**

        use template B…**4**

Flower petals: use template C*…**32**

Flower bud: use template G…**4**

Leaves:

    use template D…**4**

use template E...**4**

use template F...**4**

Stems: width of bias strips...⅞″ *Refer to Part 2 (page 111) for help, if needed.*

Flower pots: use template H...**4**

*Only one template pattern is given for flower petals. You may want to vary the shape for a more natural look.

Sashing, Center Block, Borders, and Binding

Sashing: 2½″ x 12½″ pieces...**4**

Center block:

(J) 1½″ squares...**2**

(K) 1⅞″ squares, one *each* of two fabrics...**2** *Cut in **half diagonally.***

Pieced borders:

Background:

Inner border: 3″ x 22″ pieces...**8**

Outer border: 3″ x 10″ pieces...**8**

Use template I to mark and cut angles, cutting four and four reversed, as shown.

Center block

Cutting angles

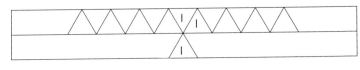

Borders

Inner border triangles: use template I...**4**

Outer border triangles: two fabrics, *each*...**two 3″ wide strips**

Then use template I to mark and cut triangles—need 32 of one and 28 of the other.

Binding: width...**3¾″**

Construction

1. Prepare the shapes for appliqué, using one of the techniques given in Part 2 (page 109) for help, if needed.
2. Make the ¼″-wide finished bias stems. You will need approximately 2 yards total. However, it does not need to be one continuous length as only shorter pieces are required. Refer to Part 2 (page 111) for help, if needed.
3. Pin, baste, and then stitch the shapes onto the background squares in the following order: stems (remember to cut them slightly longer as indicated on the pattern as other shapes will be overlapping), leaves, flower pot, flower centers, petals, and bud.
4. Make the center block, as shown.

Step 4

5. Position the blocks exactly as shown in the photo. Then join them to the sashing strips and center block.

6. Make four inner border strips, as shown.

7. Make four outer border strips, as shown.

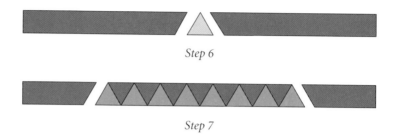

Step 6

Step 7

8. Sew the inner and outer borders together lengthwise in pairs. Then attach two borders to opposite sides. Trim the excess length as needed. Attach the borders to the top and bottom. Trim excess length as needed.

   ◆ *Helpful hint:* Use the measurement of joined blocks to determine the length of the borders.

9. Binding: Leave a ½″ extension of batting and backing beyond the edge of the quilt top to fill the wider binding. The binding corners for this quilt are straight, rather than mitered. Cut the binding into four separate lengths. Then attach the two opposite sides, trimming the ends even with the edges of the quilt top. Attach the binding strips to the remaining two sides, leaving a 1″ extension on each end to wrap around and finish the corners. Refer to Part 2 (page 119) for help, if needed.

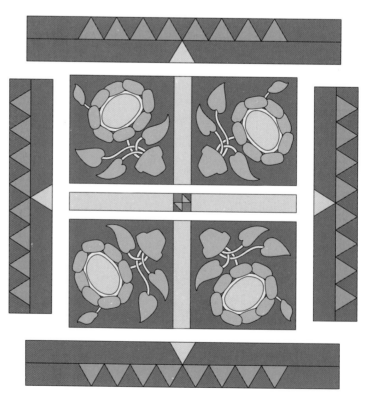

Step 8

April

WHEN Melina Elba Goyette passed away on January 7, 1976, her daughter Marie thought of the wonderful memories she had of her mother. Adorning Marie's design wall in her studio was a picture of her mother. Sharing the love of fabric her mother held as a dressmaker, Marie began to quilt. Embarking on this quilt-making journey became a departure from her teaching pottery professionally. Then, after many years of collecting fabrics—all found while searching quilt and fabric shops—Marie gathered an assortment of fabrics to make herself a quilt. Composed of large circles in various sizes, her quilt went together quickly. Marie was drawn to the picture of her mother. To her amazement, the fabric of the dress her mother was wearing was similar to many of the small prints in the quilt. A flood of emotion filled Marie and brought her sweet memories of her mother. This quilt, created with the same colors and fabrics once loved by mother and now by daughter, is indeed a miracle that defines the bonds of a mother and daughter.

April
by Marie Goyette Fritz

Traditional block pattern: Circle

FINISHED SIZE	70½″ x 70½″ *
BLOCKS SET	7 x 7
CIRCLE BLOCKS: TOTAL	49

The sashing pieces are appliquéd over the seams joining the blocks and do not add width to the quilt.

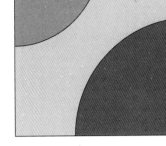

Circle block

Yardage

Backgrounds: seven fabrics, *each...***⅝**

Circles: fabrics to total...**4¼**

Appliquéd sashing strips: five fabrics, *each...***⅛**

Appliquéd posts: two fabrics, *each...***⅛**

Backing...**4¼**

Binding: ¼″ wide, finished...**½**

Post

Cutting

Blocks

Backgrounds:

   Cut 10½″-wide strips...**14** *Cut strips into 10½″ squares—need 49.*

Circles:

   Cut circles, as needed, according to size of paper pattern. (Refer to Step 1 of construction.)

Sashing, Posts, Backing, and Binding

Appliquéd sashing strips: width...**1½″** *(varying lengths from 7″ to 71″)*

Posts:

   (L) 2½″ squares...**8**

   (M) 2″ squares...**8**

Backing: lengths...**2**

   See piecing diagram (page 116) **A**

Binding: width...**1⅞″**

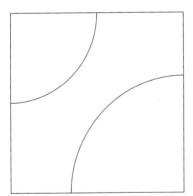

10″ block

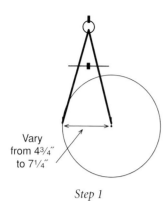

Step 1

Vary
from 4¾″
to 7¼″

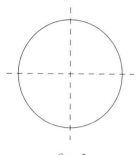

Step 2

Construction

1. Using the paper-basting method, prepare the fabric circles for appliqué. To make the paper circle patterns, use a compass to mark circles onto large pieces of paper. The distance from the centerpoint of the circle to the outer edge (radius) varies from 4¾″ to 7¼″, as shown.

2. Cut out the circles. Then fold and cut into quarters, as shown.

3. Baste the paper pattern onto the wrong side of the circle fabric, placing the corners and sides even with each other.

4. Prepare and appliqué the circles to the background fabric. Refer to Part 2 (page 109) for help, if needed.

5. Cut away the background fabric underneath the circles to within ¼″ of the stitching line. Then remove the paper pattern.

6. Arrange the blocks, and sew them together in a straight set (page 111).
   ◆ *Helpful hint:* A design wall is helpful in correctly placing the circle shapes onto the background squares.

7. Sew the lengths of sashing strips together. Turn under ¼″ and press the edges of the strips to the wrong side. Then appliqué the strips over the seams joining the blocks.

8. Appliqué the M squares onto the L squares. Then appliqué the post units to the quilt top, referring to the photograph for the exact placement.

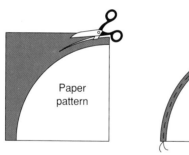

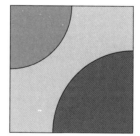

Step 4

Cherry Pie

GATHERING WITH FRIENDS *at a backyard stenciling party, Pauline fondly recalled an old quilt top from her mother's collection, one which had a bird motif with cherries in its beak. As her friends drew their favorite leaf patterns, Pauline was inspired to add her favorite emblem: the cherry. As she drew the cherries for the stencil, Pauline found herself reminiscing of the cherry pies she loved to bake, of her childhood cherry picking events, and of a childhood gingham dress appliquéd with cherries. The quilt has come to represent all those memories so dear to Pauline's heart, and so like the cherry, a self-contained refreshment center.*

Cherry Pie
by Pauline Stone Pearsall

Original cherry and bird appliqué designs, and original Cherry Pie block pattern by Pauline Stone Pearsall

CHERRY PIE

FINISHED SIZE	75″ x 75″
CHERRY PIE BLOCKS: TOTAL	64
CHERRY BLOCKS: TOTAL	77

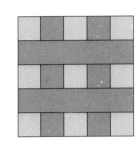

Cherry Pie block

Yardage

Light color for background: requires an additional ⅝ yard if the fabric is less
    than 44″ wide…**2½**
Assorted fabric pieces for cherries and birds, if appliquéd.
Medium color…**1**
Dark color: includes ¼″-wide binding, finished…**3¼**
Backing…**4½**

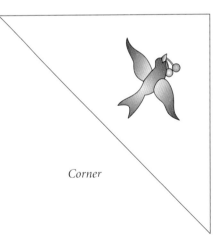

Cherry block

Cutting

The template patterns for *Cherry Pie* are on page 140.

Cherry Blocks and Corners

Background: 5½″-wide strips…**11**
    Cut strips into 5½″ squares —need 77.
Corners: 22″ squares…**2** *Cut squares in **half diagonally.***

Cherry Pie Blocks, Border, Backing, and Binding

Medium color:
    (A) 1½″-wide strips…**21**
Dark color:
    (A) 1½″-wide strips…**14**
    (B) 1½″-wide strips…**19**
        Cut B strips into 1½″ x 5½″ rectangles—need 128.
Side triangles: 9″-wide strips…**2** *Cut strips into 9″ squares—need 6.*
    *Then cut the squares into **quarters diagonally.***
Border: 5¾″-wide strips…**4**
Backing: lengths…**2**
    See piecing diagram (page 116) **A**
Binding: width…**1⅞″**

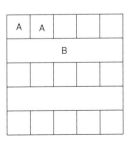

Corner

A	A			
		B		

5″ block

Construction

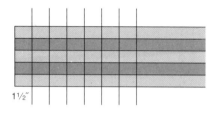

Step 1

Step 2

1. Use the 1½″-wide strips (fourteen dark and twenty-one medium-colored) to make seven sets. Then cut the sets apart every 1½″, as shown.

2. Block sew order: see diagram.

3. Using your preferred method of application, stencil or appliqué the cherries to the background squares. Refer to Part 2 (page 109) for help with appliqué, if necessary.

4. Sew the Cherry Pie blocks, Cherry blocks, and the side triangles in a diagonal set, as shown. The side triangles are cut too large in order to straighten the edges of the quilt top as needed. Trim the excess fabric to within ⅜″ of the corners of the blocks.

5. Attach the outer borders. Then use the 45° angle on your ruler to cut the correct angles, as shown.

6. Using your preferred method of application, stencil or appliqué the blackbirds to the corner triangles. Make four total (two and two reversed), referring to the photograph for placement.

7. Attach the corners to complete the quilt top. Trim and straighten the edges, if needed.

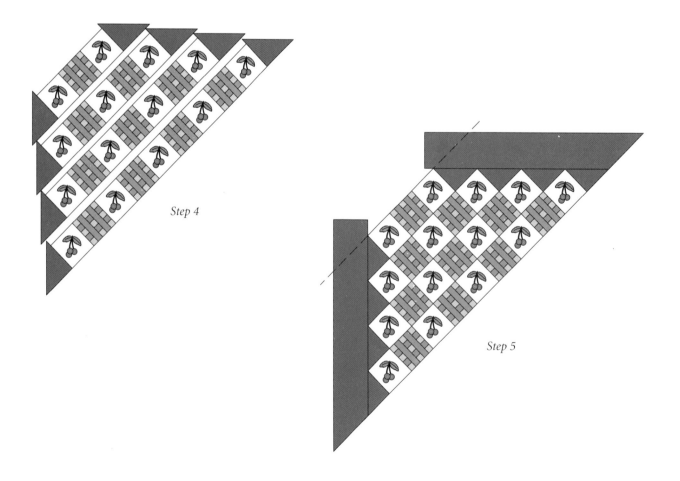

Step 4

Step 5

Kid Prints

MOLLY NOWNES was blessed with an extraordinary kindergarten teacher who demonstrated the best in teacher and child relationships. In Mrs. Bowers's class, an idea for a quilt was born by tracing the hands of each child. This special quilt let each student feel the thrill of participation. The "kid prints," which were cut from a medley of fabrics, identify each child and add a personal touch. The buses, which were cut from a mix of brightly colored yellow cottons, line the top and bottom of the quilt. This delightful quilt captures the excitement and energy of children, and the spirit of a creative classroom.

Kid Prints
by the authors

Original Schoolbus block pattern by the authors; traditional block pattern: Yankee Puzzle; quilted by Anna Venti

FINISHED SIZE	50½″ x 69½″
KID PRINT BLOCKS: TOTAL	25
SCHOOLBUS BLOCKS: TOTAL	8
YANKEE PUZZLE BLOCKS: TOTAL	16

Kid Print block

Yardage

Kid Print blocks:

> Background…**1**
>
> Assorted fabrics for handprints…**scraps**

Schoolbus blocks:

> Background: includes ¼″-wide binding, finished…**1**
>
> Bus…**eight 4½″ x 18″ pieces**
>
> Windows…**use scraps** from Kid Print background and side triangle fabric
>
> Wheels: fabrics to total…**⅛**

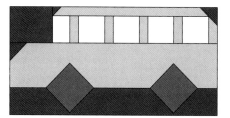

Schoolbus block

Yankee Puzzle blocks:

> Light colors: fabrics to total…**⅝**
>
> Dark colors: fabrics to total…**⅝**

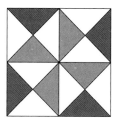

Yankee Puzzle block

Side and Corner Triangles, and Schoolbus side windows…**⅝**

Short sashing strips…**½**

Long sashing strips:

> Crosswise…**½**
>
> *or* lengthwise…**2**

Inner Border (top and bottom):

> Crosswise…**⅜**
>
> *or* lengthwise…**1½**

Fusible or transfer web…**2½**

Backing…**3¼**

6″ block

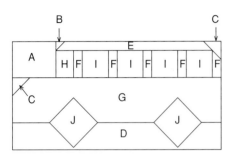

6″ x 12″ block

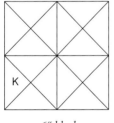

6″ block

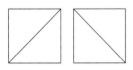

Cutting corner triangles

Cutting

Blocks

Kid Print blocks:

    Background: 6½″-wide strips…**5**

    Cut strips into 6½″ squares—need 25.

Handprint fabrics: 6″ squares…**25**

Schoolbus blocks:

    Background:

        (A) 2½″-wide strip…**1** *Cut strip into 2½″ x 3″ rectangles—need 8.*

        (B and C) 1½″-wide strip…**1** *Cut strip into sixteen 1½″ squares for C.*
            Then cut the remaining strip into eight 1″ squares for B.

        (D) 2″-wide strips…**3** *Cut strips into 2″ x 12½″ rectangles—need 8.*

    Bus fabrics, *each:*

        (E) 1″ x 10″ piece…**1**

        (F) 1″ x 2″ pieces…**5**

        (G) 3″ x 12½″ piece…**1**

    Front windows: (H) 1½″ x 2″ pieces…**8**

    Side windows: (I) 2″ squares…**32**

    Wheels: (J) 2″ squares…**16**

Yankee Puzzle blocks:

    (K) Light and dark colors, *each:*

    4¼″ squares…**32** *Cut squares into **quarters diagonally.***

Fusible or transfer web:

    6″ squares for handprints…**25**

    2″ squares for wheels…**16**

Side and Corner Triangles, Sashing, Inner Border, Backing, and Binding

Side triangles: 10½″ squares…**4** *Cut squares into **quarters diagonally.***

Corner triangles: 6½″ squares…**2** *Cut squares in **half diagonally.****

Short sashing strips:

    1½″-wide strips…**9** *Cut strips into 1½″ x 6½″ rectangles—need 50.*

Long sashing strips:

    Crosswise: 1½″ wide strips…**10**

    or lengthwise: 1½″-wide strips…**6**

    Cut to needed lengths when joining to rows of blocks.

*Alternate direction of diagonal cuts if using a directional fabric as in the diagram.

Inner horizontal border: width…**4˝**

Backing: lengths…**2**

    See piecing diagram (page 116) **B**

Binding: width…**1⅞˝**

Construction

1. Following the manufacturer's instructions, press the fusible or transfer web material to the handprint fabrics. Then trace the children's handprints onto the paper side of the fabric.

2. Cut out the handprints. Following the manufacturer's instructions, press the fabric handprints onto the right side of the background squares.
   ◆ *Helpful hint:* It is more interesting if the hands are randomly positioned. A machine buttonhole stitch was used around the handprints.

3. Have the children write their names onto the background fabric with colored permanent marking pens.

4. Yankee Puzzle blocks: sew the light and dark triangles together, as shown. Be consistent in sewing with the darker triangles on top. Then press seams toward the darker triangles.

5. Make the units, as shown.

6. Block sew order: see diagram.

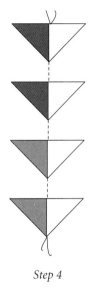

Step 4

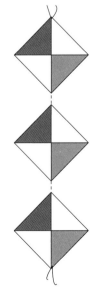

Step 5

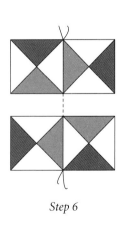

Step 6

Steps 7–8

7. Sew the side triangles, corner triangles (upper right and bottom left only), and the pieced and appliquéd blocks together in diagonal rows, joining with the short sashing strips.

8. Sew the diagonal rows together, joining with the long sashing strips, as shown. Then attach the upper left and lower right corner triangles.

9. The side and corner triangles are cut slightly too large, in order to straighten the edges of the quilt top, as needed. Trim the excess fabric to within ⅜″ of the corners of the blocks.

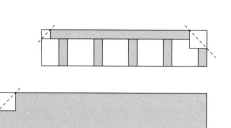

Step 10

10. Schoolbus blocks: use the double half-square triangle technique to make the units, as shown. Note one bus is facing the opposite direction. Reverse the placement of the units, as shown.

11. Block sew order: see diagram.

12. Use the fusible or transfer web material to attach the wheels to the schoolbus. Refer to the diagram for the exact placement. Stitch with a machine buttonhole stitch.

13. Attach the inner top and bottom borders.

14. Join the Schoolbus blocks to make the top and bottom borders. Then attach these borders to complete the quilt top.

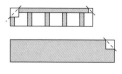
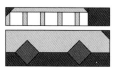

Reverse placement
Steps 10–12

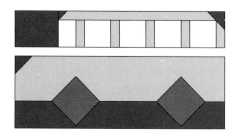

Steps 11–12

Red Tulips

RAISED IN the Pennsylvania Dutch area, Kathy Levesque finds herself drawn to memories of a peaceful lifestyle. In true German tradition, she finds comfort in the stylized hearts and tulips—they are emblems she adores. Naturally, when Kathy decided on a friendship quilt theme, she chose the traditional pattern Sister's Choice to give to her group of friends, with the instructions that they add a touch of red fabric from their personal stash. Her friends returned quickly with their blocks and Kathy began to work. Describing her work as arranging the past with a careful touch, she set the blocks together on point and the images became tulips. Kathy added appliqué tulips, a few cherries, and many meandering vines. Kathy's quilt reflects the traditional environment she enjoyed as a child.

Red Tulips
by Kathy Levesque

Traditional block pattern: Sister's Choice

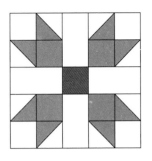

Sister's Choice block

FINISHED SIZE	66″ x 83″
SISTER'S CHOICE BLOCKS: TOTAL	18

Yardage

Background…**5¼**

Tulips (pieced and appliquéd) and cherries: fabrics to total…**1⅝**

Leaves and center squares for pieced blocks: fabrics to total…**¾**

Vine, inner border, binding (¼″ wide, finished)…**2**

Backing…**5**

Cutting

The template patterns D to J for *Red Tulips* are on page 141.

Blocks

Background:

From a 54″ length, cut crosswise:

(A) 2½″-wide strips…**5** *Cut strips into 2½″ squares—need 72.*

(B) 4½″-wide strips…**5** *Cut strips into 2½″ x 4½″ rectangles—need 72.*

(C) 2⅞″-wide strips…**6** *Cut strips into 2⅞″ squares—need 72.*
*Then cut the C squares in **half diagonally.***

Pieced tulips:

(A) 2½″-wide strips…**5** *Cut strips into 2½″ squares—need 72.*

(C) 2⅞″-wide strips…**6** *Cut strips into 2⅞″ squares—need 72.*
*Then cut the C squares in **half diagonally.***

Center square:

(A) 2½″-wide strips…**2** *Cut strips into 2½″ squares—need 18.*

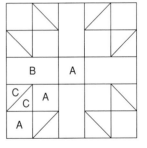

10″ block

Appliqués

Border tulips: use template D…**32**

Border corner tulips: use template F…**4**

Border leaves: use template E and ER…**32 and 32R★**

Corners leaves: use template G and GR…**4 and 4R★**

Side triangle tulip: use template H…**10**

Side triangle leaves: use template I and IR…**10 and 10R★**

Circles: use template J…**120**

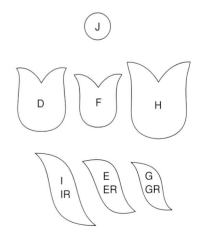

★R= reverse template on fabric

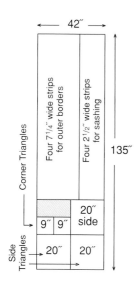

Cutting diagram

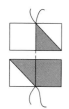

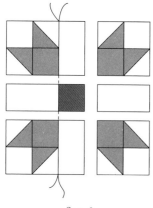

Step 2

Vines: width for ¼″-wide finished bias strips (need 24 yards)...**⅞″**

Refer to Part 2 (page 111) for help, if needed.

Side and Corner Triangles, Sashing, Borders, Backing, and Binding

From remaining light-colored background, cut pieces as shown in diagram:

Side triangles: 20″ squares...**3** *Cut squares into **quarters diagonally.***

Corner triangles: 9″ squares...**2** *Cut squares in **half diagonally.***

Outer border: width...**7¼″**

Sashing: width...**2½″**

Cut to needed lengths when joining to rows of blocks.

Inner border: width...**1½″**

Backing: number of lengths...**2**

See piecing diagram (page 116) **A**

Binding: width...**1⅞″**

Construction

1. Make the half-square triangle units for the pieced blocks using 2⅞″ triangles. Check for accuracy: each unit should measure 2½″. Refer to Part 2 (page 107) for help, if needed.

2. Unit construction and block sew order: see diagrams.

3. Sew the pieced blocks, sashing strips, and side and corner triangles together in a diagonal setting, as shown. Refer to the diagram for exact placement of sashing strips. ✦ *Helpful hint:* Use the measurement of the rows of blocks to determine the length of the sashing strips.

4. The side and corner triangles are cut slightly too large to allow for straightening the edges. Use your ruler to cut the excess fabric 1″ beyond the corners of the pieced blocks.

5. Attach the inner border. Then attach the outer border, mitering the corners of the outer border. Refer to Part 2 (page 114) for help, if needed.

6. Prepare the appliquéd shapes and vine. Refer to Part 2 (page 109) for help, if needed. ✦ *Helpful hint:* When preparing the circles, cut a template from a piece of lightweight cardboard (or a file folder). Run a small basting stitch around the edge of the fabric circle. Center the cardboard circle onto the wrong side of the fabric and pull the thread to gather. Press the seam allowance over the circle, applying a little spray sizing to set the crease. Allow the fabric to cool, and then remove the cardboard. The fabric circle is ready to be appliquéd to the quilt top. The circles in this quilt have been lightly stuffed before being appliquéd to the background.

Steps 3–4

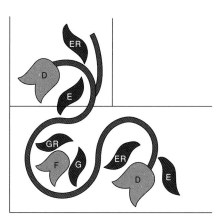

Lower left and upper right border corner appliqué placement

7. Referring to the photograph for placement, position the vines onto the background fabric. Baste and then appliqué in place. Note that some adjustment may be needed at the corners of the borders.

8. Position, pin, baste, and then appliqué the tulips, leaves, and cherries onto the background fabric, as shown. Note that the photograph shows the cherries alternate positions along the vine border.

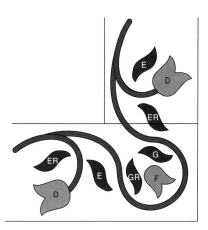

Lower right and upper left border corner appliqué placement

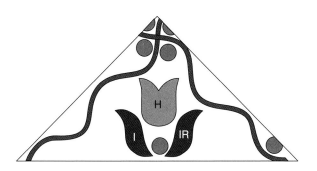

Side triangle appliqué placement

Sashing appliqué placement

Address Unknown

SELLING THE FAMILY HOME brought to the surface feelings Freddy Moran had never felt before. A restlessness surrounded her. Should we? or shouldn't we? played back and forth in her mind. Freddy's home reflected her love of life. A lifetime garden, five boys reared, a home filled with her quilt collection had left its mark. It represented her personal growth and enlightenment. Her home provided understanding of who she was and how her family lived. Yet, during this difficult time, Freddy had finished a house quilt and had sent it to the Amish community for hand quilting. After several months, Freddy sent a self-addressed envelope inquiring about the quilt. The reply from the Amish read, "mailed six weeks ago," which prompted another self-addressed envelope requesting a tracer. Unknown to Freddy, her quilt had arrived at a packaging store in her home town. But without a name or return address, the package was waiting patiently for its owner. When Freddy finally found the quilt, she exclaimed, "I can now sell the family home." The "address unknown" package was safe and sound. Freddy's restlessness disappeared, the mystery solved, and now she could move on to a new home.

Address Unknown
by Freddy Moran

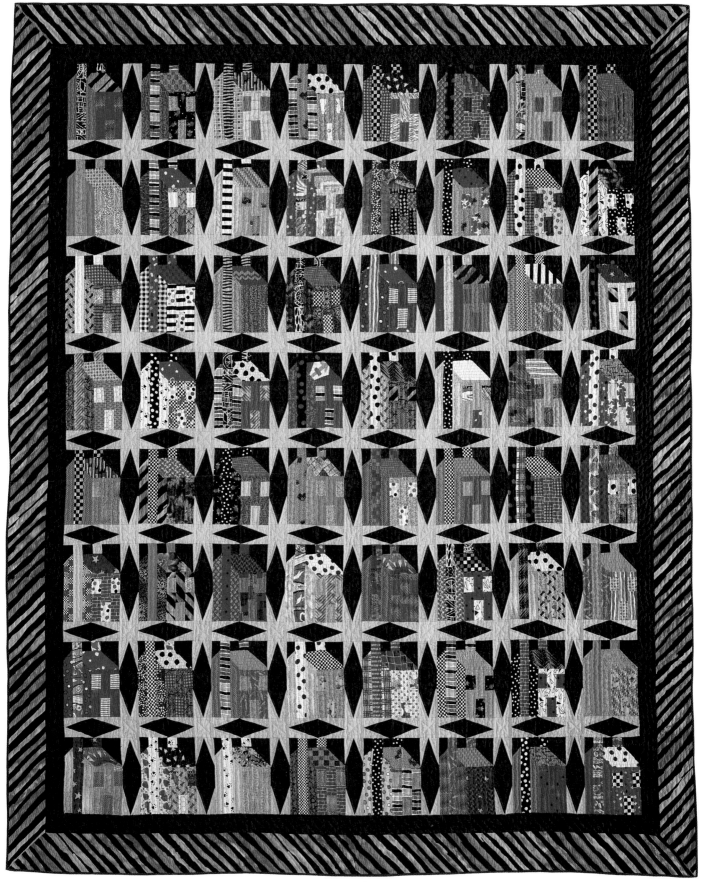

Original House block pattern by Freddy Moran; quilted by the Amish

ADDRESS UNKNOWN

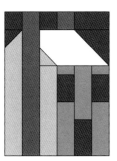

House block

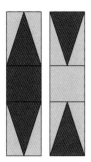

Star sashing units

FINISHED SIZE	74½″ x 90½″
BLOCKS SET	8 x 8
HOUSE BLOCKS: TOTAL	64

Yardage

Background…**3**

Stars…**1**

Houses: fabrics to total…**4¼**

Outer border:

    Crosswise…**1¼**

    or lengthwise…**2⅝**

Backing…**5½**

Binding: ¼″ wide, finished…**⅝**

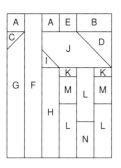

6″ x 8″ block

Cutting

The template patterns P and Q for *Address Unknown* are on page 139.

Blocks and Sashing Units

Background:

Cut inner border strips first (see below). Then from remaining 32″ width, cut crosswise:

    (A) 1½″-wide strips…**5** *Cut strips into 1½″ squares—need 128.*

    (B) 2½″-wide strips…**3** *Cut strips into 1½″ x 2½″ rectangles—need 64.*

    (C) 1½″-wide strips…**3** *Cut strips into 1½″ squares—need 64.*

    (D) 2½″-wide strips…**4** *Cut strips into 2½″ squares—need 64.*

    (O) 2½″-wide strips…**5** *Cut strips into 2½″ squares—need 56.*

    (Q) 3½″-wide strips…**12**

        Use template Q to mark and cut the angles (need 224), as shown.

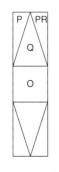

3″ x 8″ unit

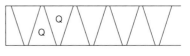

Mark with template

Star sashing units:

(O) 2½″-wide strips…**4** *Cut strips into 2½″ squares—need 49.*

(P) 3½″ wide strips…**11**

Use template P (and PR*) to mark and cut the angles (need 224 and 224R*), as shown.

Mark with template

Mark with template

Houses:

(E) 1½″ square…**1 per block**

(F) 1½″ x 8½″ piece…**1 per block**

(G) 1½″ x 7½″ piece…**1 per block**

(H) 1½″ x 5½″ piece…**1 per block**

(I) 1½″ square…**1 per block**

(J) 2½″ x 4½″ piece…**1 per block**

(K) 1″ x 1½″ pieces…**2 per block**

(L) 1½″ x 3½″ pieces…**3 per block**

(M) 1½″ x 2″ pieces…**2 per block**

(N) 1½″ x 2½″ piece…**1 per block**

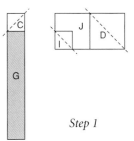

Step 1

Borders, Backing, and Binding

Inner border (background fabric):

2½″ x 90″ pieces (cut lengthwise)…**4**

Outer border: width…**4½″**

Backing: lengths…**2**

See piecing diagram (page 116) **A**

Binding: width…**1⅞″**

*R= reverse template on fabric

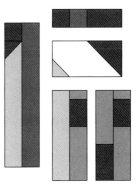

Step 2

Construction

1. Make the units using the double half-square triangle technique, as shown.
2. Block sew order: see diagram.
3. Sashing units (make 224): see diagram.
4. Vertical sashing units (make 56): see diagram.
5. Use the remaining sashing units made in Step 3 and star fabric (O) squares to make seven rows, as shown.
6. Sew the blocks together in rows, joining with the vertical sashing units.
7. Sew the rows together, joining with the horizontal sashing strips.
8. Sew the inner and outer border strips together in pairs. Then attach the borders to the quilt top. Miter the corners, referring to Part 2 (page 114) for help if needed.

Step 3

Step 4

Step 5

Miss Adams Is Going to Be a Bride

WHEN KATIE PRINDLE arrived one morning to teach an art project, the kindergarten children radiated with excitement regarding the news of their teacher: Miss Adams was going to be a bride! Katie took the opportunity to develop a special quilt for this wonderful teacher. Katie gave each child a fabric pen and let them draw on a background square of fabric their renditions of Miss Adams as a future bride. As she collected the squares, Katie saw a certain pattern developing. The little girls had drawn bridal figures amid flowers—sketches reminiscent of an entire wedding scene. The boys, however, were more cautious; they drew flower and vegetable gardens, suggesting memories of weddings with sunny days. An old-fashioned quilting bee was held, and many moms gathered to stitch together the artful blocks and borders of blue triangles. This quilt with its playful drawings and touches of blue is now a gift so dear to Mrs. McIntosh's heart.

Miss Adams Is Going to Be a Bride

by Katie Prindle, with lots and lots of helpers

Traditional block pattern: Ocean Waves; quilted by Anna Venti

Unit A

Unit B

Ocean Waves block

FINISHED SIZE	75½″ x 93½″
BLOCKS SET	7 x 9
OCEAN WAVES BLOCKS: TOTAL	63

Yardage

Background: two fabrics, *each*…**1¼**

Pieced sashing units: fabrics to total…**4½**

Border:

    Crosswise…**1¼**

    or lengthwise…**2½**

Backing…**5½**

Binding: ¼″ wide, finished…**¾**

Cutting

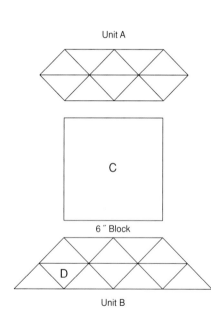

Unit A

C

6″ Block

D

Unit B

Blocks

Backgrounds:

    (C) 6½″-wide strips: two fabrics, *each*…**6**

        Cut strips into 6½″ squares—need 63.

Sashing, Border, Backing, and Binding

Pieced sashing units:

    (D) 3″-wide strips…**52** *Cut strips into 3″ squares—need 728.*

        *Then cut the squares in **half diagonally**.*

Border: width…**5″**

Backing: lengths…**2**

    See piecing diagram (page 116) **A**

Binding: width…**1⅞″**

Construction

1. Have the children draw pictures on the background squares, using permanent fabric marking pens.

2. Make 426 half-square triangle units. Refer to Part 2 (page 107) for help, if needed.

3. Make 142 sashing units, using half-square triangle units and loose triangles, as shown. Reserve 124 for the Unit A sashings.

4. Sew loose triangles to eighteen of the units made in Step 3, as shown. These are the Unit B sashings.

5. Join the blocks and sashing units in rows, as shown.

   ◆ *Helpful hint:* Do not stitch into the seam allowances when joining the blocks to the sashing units. Begin and end stitching ¼˝ from each end, as indicated by the dots in the diagram. Stitch in the direction of the arrows when joining the sashing units together.

6. Attach the border strips to complete the quilt top.

Step 3

Step 4

Step 5

Papa Marvin Jones

MARVIN JONES died with his horse in a tragic accident in the Montana mountains in September, 1995. This quilt is dedicated to Diana's grandchildren, Alexandra and Thomas McClun, who will learn about their Papa Marvin Jones through the years as fun-loving memories are recalled to mind. To share these memories of a man who was much loved and honored, Diana's daughter-in-law, Lisa, gathered quotes and sayings from her family and friends that best describe her dad. This quilt is a binding element of his life to theirs. Part of the narration in the quilt are the blocks, Fox and Geese, Right and Left, Sawtooth Star, Tree, and Country Farm. In the Bob Marshall wilderness is a plaque dedicated to Marvin Jones, which reads, "As you pass this way, kindly tip your hat to the memory of Marvin Jones, a true back-country horseman. In the Montana wilderness, he gave his life doing what he loved, serving his fellow man, and enjoying the great outdoors on horseback. May your journey be a safe one, friend!"

Papa Marvin Jones
by the authors

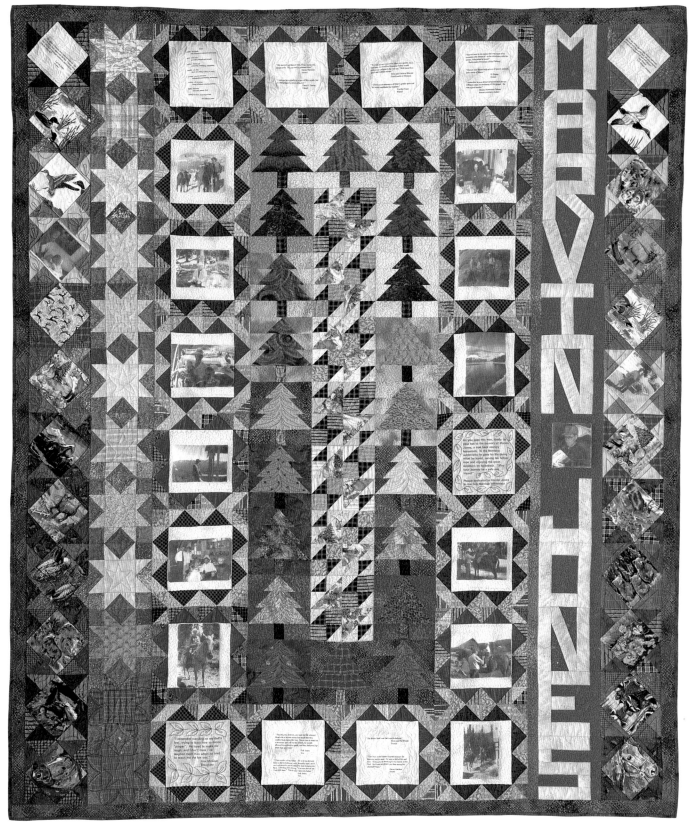

Traditional block patterns: Fox and Geese, Tree, Sawtooth Star, Right and Left, Country Farm

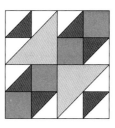

Fox and Geese

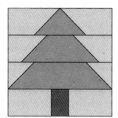

Tree

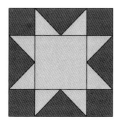

Sawtooth Star

Right and Left

Country Farm

FINISHED SIZE	63″ x 75″
FOX AND GEESE BLOCKS: TOTAL	7
TREE BLOCKS: TOTAL	20
SAWTOOTH STAR BLOCKS: TOTAL	12
RIGHT AND LEFT BLOCKS: TOTAL	24
COUNTRY FARM BLOCKS: TOTAL	20
LETTER BLOCKS: TOTAL	varies with personalization

The quilt is intended to give you ideas for personalizing your own memory quilt. If you have a theme in mind, you can choose any appropriate blocks and fabrics to carry out the theme. Your quilt may vary in size, depending upon the number of letters used. Consider a horizontal setting, or, if setting together vertically, add narrow strips of background fabric between the letters to avoid the letters running into each other. Both the photos and sayings were transferred at a T-shirt shop. The sayings were first printed from the computer and then transferred onto the fabric.

Yardage

Fox and Geese: fabrics to total…¾
Tree:
    Backgrounds: fabrics to total…**1**
    Trees: fabrics to total…¾
    Trunks: fabrics to total…⅛

Sawtooth Stars:
    Background…⅝
    Stars: fabrics to total…⅝

Right and Left:
    Backgrounds: fabrics to total…1½
    Centers: fabrics to total…½

Country Farm:
    (L) Centers…⅞
    Additional fabrics to total…2½

Letters:
    Background…⅝*
    Letters: fabrics to total…½*

Border:

Crosswise…**½**

or lengthwise…**2¼**

Backing…**4**

Binding: ¼″-wide, finished…**½**

* Yardage may vary with the number of letters used.

Cutting

Blocks

Fox and Geese blocks:

    (A) 2″ squares…**4 per block**

    (B) 2⅜″ squares…**8 per block**   *Cut the B squares in **half diagonally.***

    (C) 3⅞″ squares…**1 per block**   *Cut the C squares in **half diagonally.***

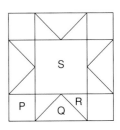

Tree blocks:

    Backgrounds: 2″-wide strips

        Cut strips into the following lengths:

        (D) 2″ x 3½″ rectangles…**2 per block**

        (E) 2″ x 2¾″ rectangles…**2 per block**

        (F) 2″ squares…**2 per block**

        (G) 2″ x 3″ rectangles…**2 per block**

    Trees: 2″-wide strips

        Cut strips into the following lengths:

        (H) 2″ x 3½″ rectangles…**1 per block**

        (I) 2″ x 5″ rectangles…**1 per block**

        (J) 2″ x 6½″ rectangles…**1 per block**

    Trunks: (K) 1½″ x 2″ rectangles…**1 per block**

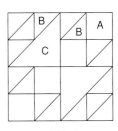

6″ block

Sawtooth Star blocks:

    Background:

        (P) 2″-wide strips…**3**   *Cut into 2″ squares—need 48.*

        (Q) 3½″-wide strips…**3**   *Cut into 2″ x 3½″ rectangles—need 48.*

    Stars:

        (R) 2″ squares…**8 per block**

        (S) 3½″ squares…**1 per block**

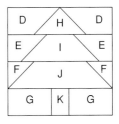

6″ block

Right and Left blocks:

    Backgrounds:

        (T) 4½″ squares…**2 per block**

        *Then cut the squares into **quarters diagonally.***

    Centers: (U) 4¾″-wide squares…**1 per block**

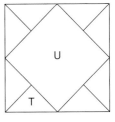

6″ block

6″ block

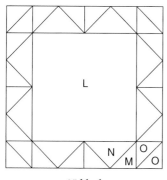

9″ block

Country Farm:

    (L) 6½″-wide strips…**4** *Cut strips into 6½″ squares—need 20.*

    (M) 2″-wide strips…**16**

        Cut strips into 2″ squares—need 16 per block, 320 total.

    (N) 3½″-wide strips…**8**

        Cut strips into 2″ x 3½″ rectangles—need 8 per block, 160 total.

    (O) 2⅜″-wide strips…**5** *Cut into 2⅜″ squares—need 80.*

    *Then cut the squares in **half diagonally.***

Letters: Refer to Part 3 (pages 123–137) for individual cutting instructions.

Background (narrow vertical sashing): 1¾″-wide strips…**2**

Border, Backing, and Binding

Border: width…**1⅞″**

Backing: lengths…**2**

    See piecing diagram (page 116) **B**

Binding: width…**1⅞″**

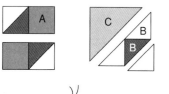

Construction

1. Make seven Fox and Geese blocks. Unit construction and block sew order: see diagrams.

2. Make 20 Tree blocks. Unit construction and block sew order: see diagrams.

3. Make 20 Country Farm blocks. Make the half-square triangle units (need four per block) and double half-square triangle units (need four per block), as shown.

Step 1

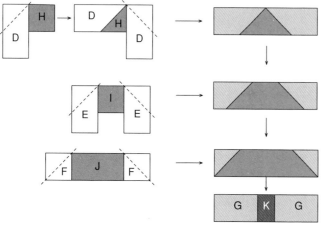

Step 2

Step 3

4. Block sew order: see diagram.

5. Make 12 Sawtooth Star blocks. Use the double half-square triangle technique (need four per block) to make units, as shown.

6. Block sew order: see diagram.

7. Make 24 Right and Left blocks. Make units (need four per block), as shown.

8. Block sew order: see diagram.

9. Make the Letters blocks, referring to Part 3 (pages 123–137) for help with construction.

10. Set the blocks together in a desired arrangement or refer to the photo for placement. Note the 1¾″-wide strips of letter background fabric are joined and then sewn to the left-hand side of the row of letters.

    ◆ *Helpful hint:* Use the measurement of the letter row to determine the length of the narrow vertical sashing strip of background fabric.

11. Attach the borders to complete the quilt top.

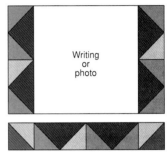

Step 4

Step 5

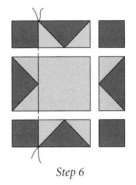

Step 6

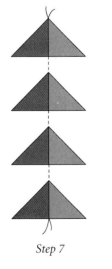

Step 7

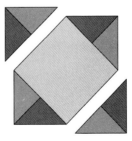

Step 8

General Techniques

ALL OF THE TECHNIQUES *needed for making any of the quilts in this book are provided in this section. Some techniques may be very familiar to you, while others may be new. Although there are many useful techniques, we have included those which work well for us when making the patterns. We feel these are the easiest, most efficient, and most accurate. We encourage you to make a practice block to become familiar with any technique, if necessary, before beginning your project. While the quick methods are indeed quick, we caution you not to be tempted to compromise precision for the sake of speed. Accuracy is most important, every step of the way!*

Fabric Preparation

There are three approaches to fabric preparation.

1. Pre-wash and pre-shrink: The fabric can be pre-washed and pre-shrunk before cutting. First, unfold and wash the lights and darks separately in a washing machine with warm water and laundry soap. (Also test for color-fastness.) Tumble dry until slightly damp, then press.

2. Pre-shrink: This process will only pre-shrink the fabric, not remove all of the chemicals. Place the unfolded fabric in a sink full of warm water. Rinse thoroughly; then, test for colorfastness. Tumble dry until slightly damp, then press.

3. Work with "new" fabric: Use the fabric as it comes off the bolt. However, it is always advisable to first test for colorfastness.

   It is a good idea to remove any chemicals from fabrics which will be used as bed quilts, especially for a baby.

Quick Cutting

Quick cutting strips and other shapes using a rotary cutter, cutting board, and wide plastic ruler is an accurate and time-saving technique.

➤ *Warning:* To prevent possible injury, check to see that the blade of your rotary cutter is sharp and without nicks, and that there are no rough edges on your wide plastic ruler. If your rotary cutter skips small sections while cutting, it is time to either sharpen or replace the blade. Refer to the manufacturer's instructions when using your rotary cutter.

1. Straighten the fabric before cutting. To do so, first press the fabric flat to eliminate the crease. Then fold the fabric in half lengthwise with selvages together, while holding it in front of you. The selvages should be even with each other and the folded edge should be without ripples. If it does ripple, slide one selvage edge to the right or left until the folded edge is smooth.

2. Place the accurately folded fabric onto the cutting board, aligning the selvages with a horizontal line on the board. Bring the folded edge even with the selvages. There are now four thicknesses and your fabric is ready for cutting. If you are working with a directional fabric such as a stripe or plaid, you may want to cut through only one thickness at a time.

3. Use the wide plastic ruler and rotary cutter to straighten the left-hand edge, as shown. Note: Instructions are for right-handed people; left-handed people should reverse the placement.

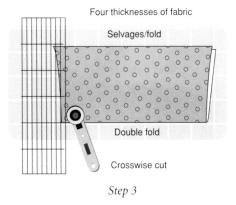

Four thicknesses of fabric

Selvages/fold

Double fold

Crosswise cut

Step 3

4. Place the marking for the desired width of the strip even with the newly cut edge of the fabric. Then use the rotary cutter to cut off a strip of fabric. ◆*Helpful hint:* Unfold the strip to see that it is without bends where the strip fabric was folded. Repress the fabric if there are bends, and then finger press the fold in the fabric.

5. Continue cutting strips the required width for the pattern you have selected.

Quick Cutting Shapes from Strips

The cutting charts in Part 1 may instruct you to cut fabric into strips and then cut the strips into other shapes, such as squares, rectangles or triangles. Refer to the following diagrams for help.

Squares:

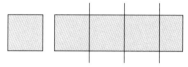

Cut strips into squares.

Rectangles:

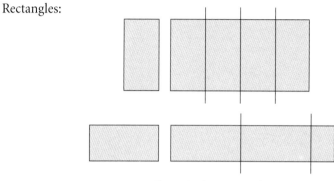

Cut strips into rectangles.

Triangles:

*Cut squares in **half diagonally.***

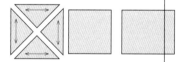

*Cut squares into **quarters diagonally.***

Piecing

Piecing is the term used for sewing individual cut shapes together to construct the pieced quilt block. Shapes can be sewn together either by hand or machine. Both methods are described on the following page.

HAND PIECING

1. Use your #8 or #9 Betweens needle and an 18" length of neutral-colored quilting thread. Do not knot the end of the thread.
2. Place two shapes right sides together. Pencil mark and then stitch a ¼" seam allowance, beginning and ending with two small backstitches and leaving tails at both ends, as shown. Then press the pieced shapes.
3. When joining additional shapes, do not stitch into the seam allowances.

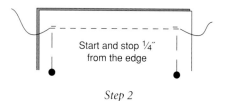

Start and stop ¼" from the edge

Step 2

MACHINE PIECING

In quiltmaking, we always use a ¼" seam allowance, which is the distance from the cut edge of the fabric to the line of stitching. An accurate ¼" seam allowance is important to the success of your pieced blocks.

Check to see that your machine is running smoothly. Use a neutral-colored 100% cotton thread in both the top and bobbin.

1. Place two shapes right sides together and stitch a ¼" seam allowance, from end to end.
2. Additional shapes can be stitched by continuing the chain of thread (called "chaining").
3. Cut the chain of thread and press the shapes.

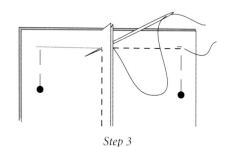

Step 3

STRIP PIECING

Fabric strips can be sewn together on the sewing machine in desired combinations. The sewn strips are then cut apart to make new units. The width of the cut strips and the distance between the cuts is determined by the individual quilt pattern.

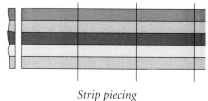

Strip piecing

HALF-SQUARE TRIANGLES

Half-square triangles are common units found in many pieced quilt block patterns. Before beginning your project, it is best to make a few sample units. If the finished units you make are consistently small, try slightly decreasing the width of the seam allowance.

1. Sew the triangles together in pairs, chaining one pair directly after the other. Do not cut the chain of threads. ◆ *Helpful hint:* Be consistent in placing the darker triangle on top when joining triangles.
2. Lay the chained units with the darker triangles facing up on a pressing board and press first on the wrong side. Then fold the darker triangle back over the stitching line and press to form a square. Cut the threads holding the pairs together and trim the extensions, as shown.
3. Check the accuracy of the units. Refer to the Checking for Accuracy section (page 108) for help, if needed.

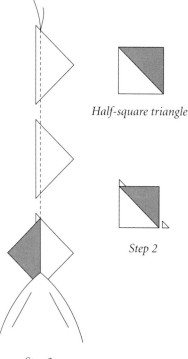

Half-square triangle

Step 2

Step 2

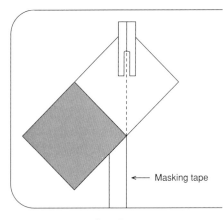

Step 1

← Masking tape

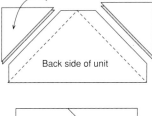

Step 3

Cut back two layers ONLY.

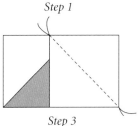

Back side of unit

Step 5

DOUBLE HALF-SQUARE TRIANGLES

Double half-square triangles are units of three triangles. Before beginning your project, it is best to make a sample unit.

1. Place a square on top of a rectangle, with right sides together. Then stitch through both thicknesses diagonally, as shown. Be very careful to stitch from corner to corner in order to keep the angle sharp. ✦ *Helpful hint:* The edge of a piece of masking tape placed directly in line with the needle, as shown, will act as a guide for stitching accurately from corner to corner. Or mark the line on your sewing machine with a permanent pen.

2. Press the top layer of fabric (the square) back over the stitching line. If the edges do not line up exactly with the rectangle, simply move your stitching line one thread width toward the outside corner.

3. With their right sides together, place another square on top of this unit. Then stitch across it diagonally, as shown.

4. Press the square fabric back over the stitching line. Check to see that all the edges of the squares and rectangle are even with each other. Use the rectangle as your guide for an accurate finished unit.

5. Trim off the excess fabric (cut only the two layers of fabric behind the triangles) to within ¼″ of the stitching lines, as shown. Then press.
   ✦ *Helpful hint:* This technique can be applied to shapes other than rectangles. For example, it is used to add triangular corners to the Apple, Cup and Saucer, and Heart blocks (pages 124, 125, and 127).

Pressing

Pressing is an important part of quiltmaking. Get in the habit of pressing often as you sew.

Set your iron on the cotton setting. Use a well-padded pressing surface, such as an ironing board covered with a light-colored mat. ✦ *Helpful hint:* A dense, short nap such as a bath mat works well. The mat acts to keep the shapes from slipping on the board and also prevents the seam allowance from creating a ridge on the right side of the block.

Press the seam allowance flat on the wrong side first to flatten the machine stitches, then on the right side. Whenever possible, press the seam allowance in the direction of the darker fabric. Allow the fabric to cool before removing it from the pressing surface to avoid possible distortion. Use spray sizing if desired to finish the block.

Checking for Accuracy

Whether you call it "truing up," "squaring up," or "trimming off," it is important to check the accuracy of your units before incorporating them into the pieced block.

CHECKING HALF-SQUARE TRIANGLE UNITS

1. With the right side facing you, place the half-square triangle unit onto the cutting board. (The ruler we like best for this step is a clear plastic 6″ square with a 3″ one-eighth grid square in one corner.) Lay the clear plastic ruler over the unit, with the diagonal marking directly over the seam line. If, for example, you need to square the unit to 3″, the 3″ marking on the left-hand side and bottom edge of the ruler should be either directly on the edges of the unit or inside the unit, not beyond the edge of the fabric. When the ruler is correctly positioned, check to see if there is any fabric extending beyond the edge of the ruler on the right-hand side and the top edge. If there is, use the rotary cutter to trim it off, as shown.

2. Turn the unit 90° and repeat the process. The unit should now measure exactly 3″. ◆ *Helpful hint:* This step is also helpful when checking the accuracy of other units, such as four-patches and double half-square triangles.

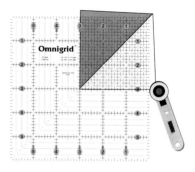

Step 1

Appliqué

Included in this section are three methods of preparing your motif for either hand or machine appliqué.

PAPER BASTING WITH FREEZER PAPER

Use the plastic-coated freezer paper that can be purchased at your local grocery store.

1. Carefully trace the motif from the template patterns on pages 139–143 onto the paper side of the freezer paper. If you plan to hand appliqué, the paper patterns can often be re-used. However, if you will be machine appliquéing, you will need one pattern for each shape. Use paper scissors to cut out the shapes. ◆ *Helpful hint:* The freezer paper can be folded to cut multiple shapes.

2. With the paper side facing you, lay the freezer paper pattern onto the wrong side of the fabric. Use a dry iron to press the paper shapes to the fabric.

3. Cut out the fabric shape ¼″ larger than the freezer paper pattern all the way around. Turn the ¼″ allowance to the wrong side and hand baste around the edges. Press the shape. The shape is now ready to be appliquéd either by hand or machine to the background fabric. Refer to the section following on either hand or machine appliqué.

4. After the shape has been stitched to the background fabric, carefully cut and remove the background fabric to within ¼″ of the stitching line.

5. Peel off the paper pattern.

NEEDLE TURN WITH FREEZER PAPER

Freezer paper pressed to the right side of each motif acts as a guideline for turning under the allowance. Use plastic-coated freezer paper that can be purchased at your local grocery store.

1. Carefully trace the motif from the template patterns on pages 139–143 onto the paper side of the freezer paper. If you plan to hand appliqué, the paper patterns can often be re-used. However, if you will be machine appliquéing, you will need one pattern for each shape. Use paper scissors to cut out the shapes. ◆ *Helpful hint:* The freezer paper can be folded to cut multiple shapes.

2. With the right side facing up, place the fabric on the pressing surface. With the paper side up, place the freezer paper pattern onto the fabric. If cutting multiple shapes, leave at least ½″ between each shape.

3. Use a dry iron to press the paper shapes to the fabric, pressing firmly and carefully to avoid ripples.

4. With your fabric scissors, cut the shapes apart ⅛″ beyond the edges of the paper pattern.

5. With the paper side face up, place the cut shape onto the background in the desired position. Pin or baste in place to the background.

6. Thread your Betweens needle with a single strand of thread in a color to match the motif. Secure one end with a knot.

7. Use the tip of your needle to turn the edges of the motif under ⅛″, using the edge of the freezer paper as a guide. Hold it in place with the thumb of your free hand.

8. Using a small back whipstitch, appliqué the motif to the background fabric. Refer to the following Hand Appliqué section for help with the back whipstitch.

9. Remove the basting stitches. Then carefully peel off the freezer paper from the front side.

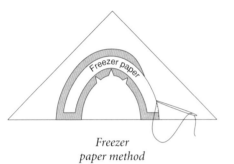

*Freezer
paper method*

FUSIBLE OR TRANSFER MATERIAL

This method of preparing shapes is quick and easy. The finished look is flat and the edges of the shapes are often buttonhole stitched either by hand or machine. There are several fusible bonding materials available and it is best to experiment with different weights.

1. Mark or trace the shape onto the paper side of the bonding fabric.

2. Follow the manufacturer's instructions for bonding the fusible material to the wrong side of your fabric. Use paper scissors to cut out the shapes.

3. Follow the manufacturer's instructions for removing the paper backing. Then fuse the fabric shape onto the background fabric.
   Optional: Use a hand or machine buttonhole stitch around the edges of the shape.

HAND APPLIQUÉ

The preferred stitch used for hand appliqué is a back whipstitch. This is a good holding stitch for keeping the shape taut against a background fabric. Using a single strand of thread in a color to match the motif, secure one end with a knot. Bring the needle and thread up from the underside and out through the folded edge in the motif. Insert the tip of the needle a little below and slightly under the folded edge where the thread emerges. Without pulling the thread through, slant the needle and bring it to the top side through the folded edge in the motif, approximately $1/16''$ away from the previous stitch. Pull the thread through. Keep the tension even, neither too loose nor too tight. Continue stitching. End with two small backstitches on the back side.

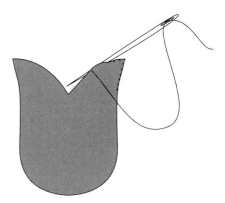

Back whipstitch

MACHINE BUTTONHOLE STITCH APPLIQUÉ

It is always advisable to sew on a test piece first. Make any necessary adjustments in stitch length or width and determine the proper position of the foot along the edge of the motif.

MAKING VINES OR STEMS

One method for making stems and vines uses bias bars or $1/4''$ flat metal strips.

1. Cut a bias strip of fabric $7/8'' \times 25''$ from a $1/2$ yard of fabric.
2. Fold the bias strip in half lengthwise with the wrong sides together.
3. Machine stitch along the lengths with an accurate $1/8''$ seam allowance to create a tube.
4. Insert the metal strip into the fabric tube, placing the seam line in the center of the flat side of the bar.
5. With the metal strip still inserted in the fabric tube, press on both sides of the fabric.
6. Remove the metal strip. The fabric tubes are now ready to be appliquéd to the background fabric.

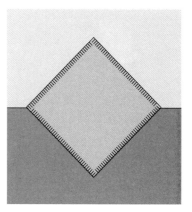

Machine buttonhole stitch

Settings

STRAIGHT SETTING

A straight setting means that blocks are sewn together in straight horizontal and vertical rows.

Sewing Blocks Together

1. With the first block in each row on top, stack the blocks from Row 1 and Row 2, as shown. ◆ *Helpful hint:* Mark the number of each row onto a piece of paper to eliminate any mix-up.
2. Place the top block from Rows 1 and 2 right sides together. Stitch the blocks together along the right-hand edge.

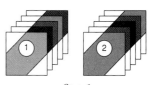

Step 1

Steps 2–4

3. Continue the chain of thread and sew the second set of blocks in Rows 1 and 2 together along the right-hand edge.

4. Continue chaining the remaining pairs of blocks from Rows 1 and 2 together in the same manner. Do not cut the chain of threads holding the pairs.

5. With the first block on top, stack the blocks in Row 3. Then, with their right sides together, stitch them to the blocks in Row 2, using the same method of chaining between rows. Repeat this procedure for the remaining rows.

6. Press the new seams in each horizontal row in opposite directions, as shown, to prevent bulk when you join the rows.

7. Sew the horizontal rows together, placing pins at the intersections of their seams.

8. Press the new seams to one direction.

9. Give the quilt top a final press.

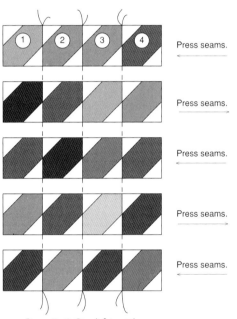

Steps 5–6, Straight setting

Straight setting with horizontal sashing

Adding Sashing and Posts to a Straight Setting

When only adding either horizontal or vertical sashing strips to a straight setting, such as in *Cups & Saucers* (page 53) and *Grandmother's Choice* (page 21), it is extremely important that the length of each sashing strip be the same, otherwise the finished quilt top may be askew. You may need to ease the rows of pieced blocks to fit the sashing strips. However, any slight discrepancy can easily be distributed along the entire length of the strip.

Take an accurate measurement through the center of the rows of blocks, either horizontal or vertical. Then use an average measurement to determine the cut length of the sashing strips.

When the sashing strips are joined at the intersections by posts, such as in *Grammy's Goose* (page 62), all of the sashing strips (both horizontal and vertical) are cut the same length. Sew the blocks to the sashing strips and posts, as shown.

DIAGONAL SETTING

A diagonal setting means that blocks are turned "on point" and sewn together in diagonal rows. Side and corner triangles are required when using this setting. The cut sizes of all of the side and corner triangles for the patterns in this book are deliberately cut slightly too large. This will allow you to trim the excess and straighten the edges before adding borders or binding.

Sewing Blocks Together

1. Lay out all of the quilt blocks and side and corner triangles on the floor or on your design wall. ◆ *Helpful hint:* Mark the number of each row onto a piece of paper to eliminate any mix-up.
2. Sew the side triangles to opposite sides of the block in Row 1, as shown.

Step 2

3. Stitch together the side triangles and the blocks in Row 2.
4. Stitch together the blocks and side triangles in the remaining rows in the same manner.
5. Join Row 1 to Row 2, alternating the direction of the seams and placing pins at the seam intersections to hold them secure.
6. Add Row 3, Row 4, etc. Then sew on the four corner triangles.
7. Take the quilt top to the cutting board. Use the wide plastic ruler and rotary cutter to straighten the edges of the quilt top and remove the excess fabric to within ⅜″ of the corners of the blocks. When adding a border or binding, allow ⅜″ rather than the usual ¼″. This will prevent you from cutting off the corner points of the blocks. Check to see that the opposite sides are the same measurement and that corners make accurate 90° angles. Be careful not to stretch the edges.
8. Give the quilt top a final press.

Straight setting with horizontal and vertical sashing

Straight setting with sashing and posts

Step 6, Diagonal setting

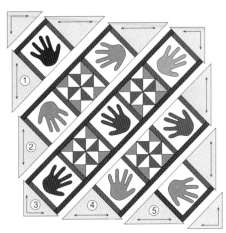

Diagonal setting with sashing

Steps 2–3

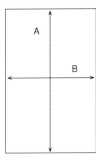

Measuring borders

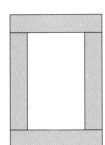

Straight borders

Adding Sashing Strips to a Diagonal Setting

A design wall is very helpful when determining the placement of the blocks, sashing strips, and side and corner triangles for this setting. All of the short sashing strips will be cut the same length, which is the same measurement as the unfinished blocks. The length of the longer sashing strips are easier to determine and cut as you go.

1. When all of the blocks and side triangles are arranged on your design wall, determine the number of short sashing strips needed. Refer to the diagram for help. ✦ *Helpful hint:* Mark the number of each row onto a piece of paper to eliminate any mix-up.
2. Sew short sashing strips to opposite sides of the block in Row 1, as shown.
3. Measure the distance across this unit to determine the length of the longer sashing strip. Stitch it to the upper edge, as shown.
4. Sew the short sashing strips, long sashing strips, then side triangles, using the same method as described above, for the remaining rows. Refer to the diagram for help. Note that the center row will have a long sashing strip on both the top and bottom.
5. Join the diagonal rows, placing pins to keep the short sashing strips aligned.
6. Sew the corner triangles to complete the quilt top.
7. Refer to Step 7 of Sewing Blocks Together (page 113) to trim the excess and straighten the edges.

Borders

Border strips can be a single strip of fabric cut on the lengthwise grain or they can be pieced from strips cut on the crosswise grain. In this book yardage has been given for both types of cutting. Whichever direction you are cutting the strips for the borders, it is best to first remove the selvage edges. The width of the strips is given in the yardage charts.

If you plan to add a border to your quilt top, it is important to accurately determine the length of the border strips. ➤ *Warning:* Do not simply sew the border strips to the quilt top without first measuring. If you do, you could have rippled edges or splayed corners.

MEASURING BORDERS

Lay the quilt top on a flat surface and use a plastic or metal tape measure to determine dimension A and dimension B across the center from edge to edge. Write these measurements down. This is more accurate than measuring the sides, where stretching can occur.

STRAIGHT BORDERS

Attaching Straight Borders

1. Cut two strips of fabric for the borders the desired width (plus ½″ for seam allowance) by the measurement determined above for dimension A.

2. Place pins at the center points of the border strips and also at the center points along the corresponding sides of the quilt top, as shown.

3. Lay these border strips right sides together with the quilt top, matching pins at the center points and placing pins at opposite ends to hold secure. Place additional pins along the length, evenly distributing any fullness if necessary.

4. Sew with the border strips on top, as they are more stable than the quilt top and less likely to stretch.

5. Press the border strips flat on the wrong side. Then fold them over the stitching lines and press.

6. Lay the quilt top on a flat surface. Measure to determine the new dimension B (which includes the attached border strips).

7. Cut two strips of fabric the desired width (plus ½″ for seam allowance) by the measurement determined in Step 6.

8. Place pins at the center points of the border strips and the quilt top, as shown. Then attach these strips to the quilt top, using the same method described in Steps 3-5.

9. Additional straight borders can be added, following the same method described in Steps 1-8.

10. Give the quilt top a final press.

MITERED BORDERS

Attaching Mitered Borders

1. Using the figure determined in the Measuring Borders section, cut two strips of fabric the measurement of dimension A plus two times the cut width of the border. Then add an additional 4″ for working allowance. It is always important to have extra border length for mitering corners, so don't be too skimpy.

2. Repeat the same procedure of measuring and cutting strips for dimension B.

3. Place pins at the center points of the two border strips. Measure out from the pins in each direction a distance equal to one-half the A dimension. Place pins at these points to mark the corners. Also place pins at the center points along the corresponding sides of the quilt top, as shown.

4. With right sides together, lay the border strips on the corresponding sides of the quilt top. Match pins with the corners and at the center points. Use more pins to hold the borders in place. Beginning and ending ¼″ from each corner, stitch the border strips to the quilt top with the border strip on top, as it is more stable than the quilt top and less likely to stretch. Evenly distribute any fullness if necessary.

5. Mark the center points on the other two border strips. From both directions, measure one-half the B dimension. Mark those points with pins.

6. Pin the center points along the corresponding sides of the quilt top. Then sew these borders to the quilt top, as in Step 4.

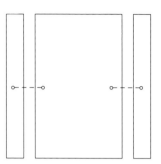
Step 2

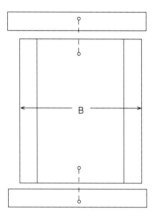
Steps 6–8

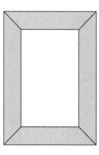
Mitered borders

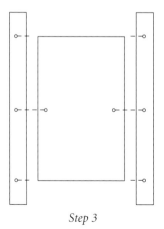
Step 3

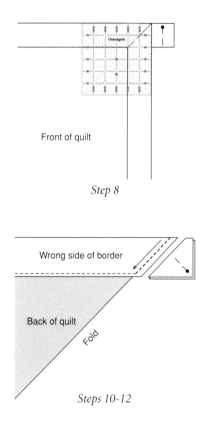

Front of quilt

Step 8

Wrong side of border

Back of quilt

Fold

Steps 10-12

7. Working on one corner of the quilt at your pressing surface, bring the unsewn border ends out straight, overlapping the end of one over the end of the other.

8. Lift the strip and fold it at a 45° angle under only itself. Use your ruler to check that the corner is square and the angle is 45°, as shown. Then press to set.

9. On the wrong side, place pins near the pressed fold in the corner to secure the border strips.

10. With the wrong side up, stitch along the folded line in the corner. To avoid gaps or puckers, carefully stitch only to the previous stitching line.

11. Trim the excess fabric from the borders, as shown. Then press on the right side.

12. Miter the other corners, following the same method described in Steps 7-11.

Backing Fabric

Quiltmakers are becoming more and more creative with the backs of their quilts. Leftover lengths of borders can be stitched together and even extra blocks can be incorporated into the backing. It is always fun to turn a quilt to its "wrong" side and be surprised by the backing. The backing fabric should be at least 2″ larger all the way around than the quilt top. Remember to remove the selvage edges as they are tightly woven and difficult to quilt through.

Below are suggested piecing diagrams for the backs of the quilts in this book. The project cutting charts will refer to the one that is best suited for the quilt you are making. After joining lengths of strips, press the seams *open* since open seams are easier to quilt through.

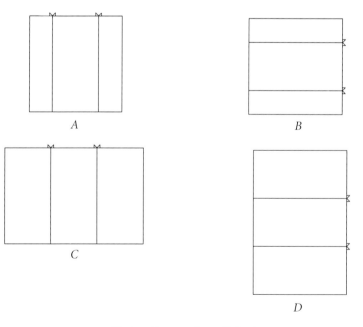

A

B

C

D

Piecing diagrams for quilt backs

Layering and Basting for Hand Quilting

Use a large utility table (or tables) or the floor for this process, as the needle will scratch the surface and mark a dining table. *Note:* If you will be hand quilting in a frame, you may be able to skip this process and proceed directly to the quilting. Just follow the manufacturer's instructions which accompany your frame. If you will be using a hoop, proceed as follows:

1. With the wrong side facing you, lay the backing on the table or floor. Secure with masking tape. Be sure that the backing is held taut.

2. Lay the batting on top of the backing. Smooth out any folds or creases. Use a paper scissors to trim any excess.

3. With the right side facing you, center the quilt top over the batting. Carefully smooth it flat.

4. Starting in the center and working out toward the edges, use glass-head pins to secure all three layers, placing pins approximately 6″ apart.

5. Thread a darning needle with approximately 4 feet of light-colored thread (quilting thread works well). Secure one end with a knot.

6. Starting from the center of the quilt and working toward the edges, stitch the layers together with a long diagonal basting stitch, as shown. The stitches should form a grid approximately 6″ apart, as shown.

7. Remove the pins and masking tape. Trim the batting to within ½″ of the quilt top.

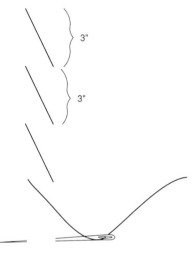

Diagonal basting stitch

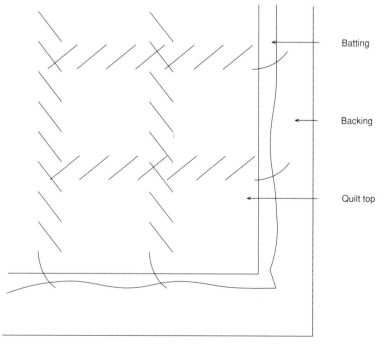

Basting in a 6″ grid

8. Trim the backing to within 2″ of the quilt top. Then fold the excess backing in half, so that the raw edge of the backing comes up even with the edge of the quilt top. Fold the backing again, bringing the fold of the backing over the quilt top ¼″. Use a long running stitch to sew the folded edge through all layers. This is *not* the finished edge of the quilt. A separate binding will be attached when the quilting is done.

Hand Quilting

THE QUILTING STITCH

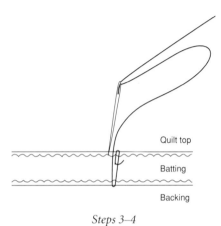

Quilt top

Batting

Backing

Steps 3–4

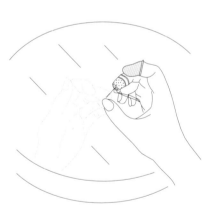

Step 5

1. Thread your small Betweens needle with quilting thread (approximately 18″ long), which has a knot in one end.
2. Place a thimble on the center finger of your quilting hand and a finger cot on the pointer finger of the same hand. ✦ *Helpful hint:* Finger cots can be purchased at your local drug store or quilting store. They are useful as grabbers for pulling the needle and thread through the three layers.
3. Insert the needle and thread, going through only the batting layer, and come up at the point where you want to start quilting. Then gently tug on the thread to pop the knot into the batting layer.
4. Take a small backstitch. Then place the tip of the center finger of your free hand on the backside of the quilt, directly under the area to be quilted.
5. Insert the tip of the needle straight down into the quilt and push through with your thimble. As soon as the tip touches your finger, immediately bring the tip of the needle up to the front side. To do this, position the thumb of your quilting hand approximately 1″ ahead of the point where the needle is inserted. Then pressing your thumb against the quilt and pushing the needle at an upward angle with your thimble finger, bring the tip of the needle up. As soon as the tip of the needle is visible, insert it again through all layers, just a little ahead of where it came up. Continue with this "up-and-down" rocking motion until there are about four stitches on the tip of your needle. Then bring the needle and thread all the way through. Continue stitching across the line in the same manner.
6. To end the thread, take a small backstitch through the top layer only. Pull the needle and thread to the top side. Wrap the thread around the needle twice. While holding the wraps with your free hand, pull the needle through. This will create a French knot close to the surface of the quilt. At the point where the thread emerged, insert the needle into the batting layer and gently tug to pop the knot below the surface of the quilt top. Bring the needle and thread out about ½″ away, and cut the thread.

Layering and Basting for Machine Quilting

1. Follow Steps 1 through 3 of Layering and Basting for Hand Quilting (page 117). Then use safety pins to secure all three layers, placing pins approximately 3″ to 4″ apart. Avoid placing pins directly over seams or areas that will receive quilting lines.
2. Trim the batting to within 1″ of the quilt top.

Machine Quilting

Two styles of quilting are done on the sewing machine: straight line and free motion. Straight-line quilting consists of all the straight lines on the quilt, including diagonals. To prevent slipping and puckering, use a walking foot on your sewing machine for straight-line quilting.

Free-motion quilting allows you to stitch around curves and make free-form designs as in stippling. Lower (or cover) the feed dogs on your sewing machine, bringing the bobbin thread to the top side. Then with the area to be quilted directly under the foot, take small stitches in place to form a knot. Cut the thread tail. Move the quilt in order to stitch around the curved designs.

Binding

PREPARATION FOR BINDING

1. Run a long machine basting stitch ⅛″ from the edge of the quilt top all the way around.
2. Using the rotary cutter and board, remove the excess batting and backing even with the edge of the quilt top. If your finished binding will be wider than ¼″ you will want to leave a small extension of batting and backing.

CUTTING BINDING STRIPS

The fabric you are using for the binding may determine the direction you wish to cut it. For example, some directional prints are more pleasing if cut lengthwise, following the printed pattern; other fabrics are just fine cut on the crosswise grain. Generally, we reserve bias binding for quilts that have curved edges. However, many plaids and stripes are very attractive when cut and sewn on the bias, as in the *Peggy's Baskets* quilt (page 49). Cut the binding strips the width indicated in the individual quilts in Part 1.

ATTACHING CONTINUOUS BINDING STRIPS

1. Sew lengths of binding strips together to extend around the entire edge of the quilt plus 8″.
2. Fold the starting end of the binding strip at a 45° angle, as shown. Then, with the right side facing out, fold the binding strip in half lengthwise and press. Apply spray sizing to give stability and set the crease.

Wrong side

Fold up.

Step 2

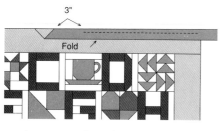

Steps 3–5

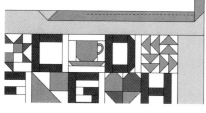

Step 6

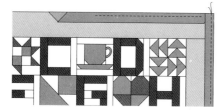

Steps 7–8

3. With their right sides together and raw edges even, lay the binding strip on the quilt.

   ✦ *Helpful hint:* Avoid placing a binding strip seam at a corner. Make a trial run with the binding strip around the edge of the quilt to determine an appropriate starting point; do *not* start at a corner.

4. Starting 3″ from the beginning of the binding strip, stitch the binding to the quilt ¼″ from the edge of the quilt top, as shown. ✦ *Helpful hint:* A walking foot on your sewing machine is helpful in maintaining even tension while attaching the binding.

5. Continue stitching to within ¼″ of the corner. Then stop and backstitch. Remove the quilt from the machine.

6. Lay the corner of the quilt on a flat surface and fold the binding strip away from the quilt, as shown.

7. Fold the binding strip toward you, the top folded edge even with the top edge of the quilt top, and the raw edges even with the right-hand side of the quilt, as shown. Pin to secure.

8. Starting at the top folded edge of the binding strip, stitch along the length to within ¼″ of the next corner. Stop and backstitch.

9. Remove the quilt from the machine. Repeat Steps 6-8.

10. When you have come to within 4″ of the starting point, stop and remove the quilt from the machine. Slip the end of the binding strip into the starting end. Trim any excess length if necessary. Pin to secure.

11. Stitch the final section of binding to the quilt.

12. Finger press the binding strip up and over the edge of the quilt to the back, folding the binding at the corners to form miters on both the front and back. Pin to hold in place on the back. Use a hand slipstitch to secure the folded edge of the binding to the back of the quilt.

Alphabet Sampler

YEARS AGO, *samplers were the teaching tools for young girls learning to embroider. These "students" would learn the alphabet while perfecting their stitches. Today the quilted sampler is a tool to teach beginners an assortment of blocks from A to Z. This quilt is our tribute to those bygone years. The quilt brings to life the samplers of the alphabet with blocks that correspond to each letter. You can personalize your quilts with your name, or use the alphabet blocks in other projects. To encourage beginning students, the* Alphabet Sampler *quilt is offered to all quilters as a sampler for the classroom.*

Alphabet Sampler
by the authors

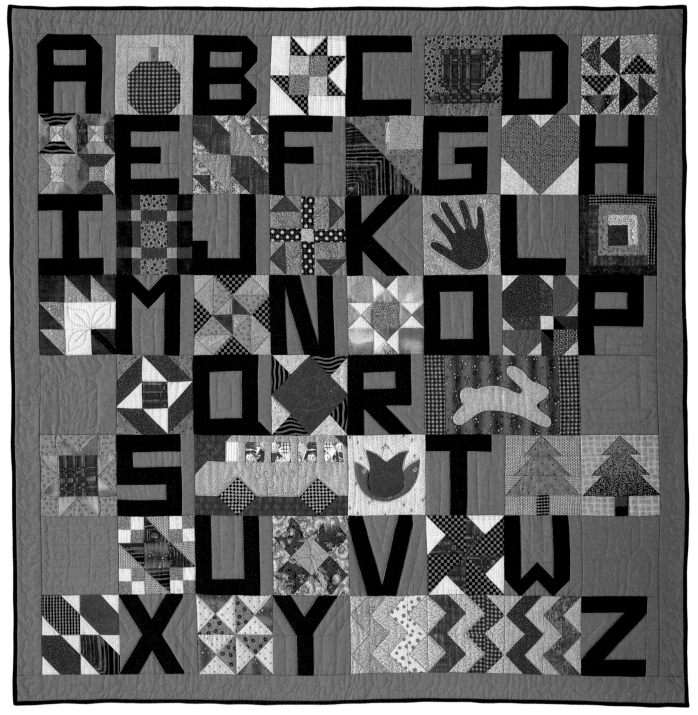

Machine quilted by Kathy Sandbach

FINISHED SIZE   52½″ x 52½″

Yardage

Letter blocks:

    Background: includes Plain blocks and border…**1¾**

    Letters: includes binding…**1½**

Pieced blocks…**variety of fabrics**

Backing…**3¼**

Cutting and Construction

General Instructions

1. Refer to Part 2 (page 108) for the double half-square triangle technique (DHST) in the block construction for help, if needed.

2. Attach the angled pieces of letters K, N, R, V, X, Y, and Z to the background piece, pressing the seam allowances along the lengths to the wrong side. Position the pieces on the background, overlapping the edges if needed, as shown in the placement diagram. Trim the excess. Topstitch the piece in place, and sew the block units together.

3. Join the letter blocks and the pieced blocks together in a straight set, referring to the photograph for placement.

4. Attach the borders to complete the quilt top.

Letter Blocks

Background:

    1½″-wide strips…**6**

    1⅝″-wide strip…**1**

    1¾″-wide strip…**1**

    2⅜″-wide strip…**1**

    2⅞″-wide strip…**1**

    3″-wide strip…**1**

    4¼″-wide strip…**1**

    5½″-wide strip…**1**

Letters:

    1¾″-wide strips…**12**

ALPHABET BLOCKS

A. APPLE

B. BABY BUNTING

C. CUP AND SAUCER

D. DUTCHMAN'S PUZZLE

E. EMPTY SPOOLS

F. FOX AND GEESE

G. GRANDMOTHER'S CHOICE

H. HEART

I. INTERWOVEN

J. JACK IN THE BOX

K. KID PRINT

L. LOG CABIN

M. MAPLE LEAF

N. NEXT-DOOR NEIGHBOR

O. OHIO STAR

P. PANSY

Q. QUARTERED STAR

R. RABBIT
    RIGHT AND LEFT

S. SAWTOOTH STAR
    SCHOOLBUS

T. TULIP
    TREE

U. UNDERGROUND RAILROAD

V. VEGETABLE SOUP

W. WHIRLWIND

X. X-QUISITE

Y. YANKEE PUZZLE

Z. ZIGZAG

Plain Blocks, Border, Backing, and Binding

Plain blocks: 6½″ squares…**4**

Border: width…**2½″**

Backing: lengths…**2**

　　See piecing diagram (page 116) **A**

Binding: width…**1⅞″**

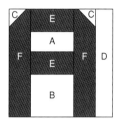

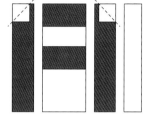

A, 6″ block

Background:

　　(A) one 1⅝″ x 3″ rectangle

　　(B) one 2⅞″ x 3″ rectangle

　　(C) two 1½″ squares

　　(D) one 1½″ x 6½″ rectangle

Letter:

　　(E) two 1¾″ x 3″ rectangles

　　(F) two 1¾″ x 6½″ rectangles

Use the DHST to attach the C squares to the F rectangles.

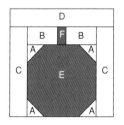

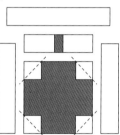

Apple, 6″ block

Background:

　　(A) four 1½″ squares

　　(B) two 1½″ x 2¼″ rectangles

　　(C) two 1½″ x 5½″ rectangles

　　(D) one 1½″ x 6½″ rectangle

Apple:

　　(E) one 4½″ square

Stem:

　　(F) one 1″ x 1½″ rectangle

Use the DHST to attach the A squares to the E square.

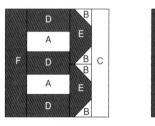

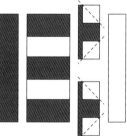

B, 6″ block

Background:

　　(A) two 1⅝″ x 3″ rectangles

　　(B) four 1½″ squares

　　(C) one 1½″ x 6½″ rectangle

Letter:

　　(D) three 1¾″ x 3″ rectangles

　　(E) two 1¾″ x 3½″ rectangles

　　(F) one 1¾″ x 6½″ rectangle

Use the DHST to attach the B squares to the E rectangles.

Background:

    (A) one 2″ square

    (B) four 2″ x 3½″ rectangles

    (E) one 3⅞″ square, cut in ***half diagonally***

Baby Bunting:

    (A) four 2″ squares, two each of two fabrics

    (C) four 2″ squares

    (D) one 2⅜″ square, cut in ***half diagonally***

Use the DHST to attach the C squares to the B rectangles.

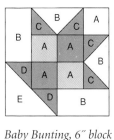 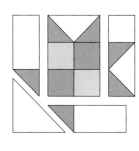

Baby Bunting, 6″ block

Background:

    (A) one 4″ x 4¼″ rectangle

    (B) one 1½″ x 6 ½″ rectangle

Letter:

    (C) two 1¾″ x 4¼″ rectangles

    (D) one 1¾″ x 6½″ rectangle

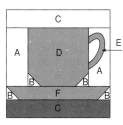

C, 6″ block

Background:

    (A) two 1¾″ x 3¾″ rectangles

    (B) four 1¼″ squares

    (C) one 1½″ x 6½″ rectangle

Cup and Saucer:

    (D) one 3¾″ x 4″ rectangle

    (E) one with template (page 139)

    (F) one 1¼″ x 6½″ rectangle

Shelf:

    (C) one 1½″ x 6½″ rectangle

Use the DHST to attach the B squares to rectangles D and F.

 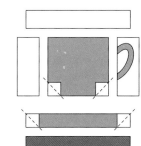

Cup and Saucer, 6″ block

Background:

    (A) one 3″ x 4″ rectangle

    (B) two 1½″ squares

    (C) one 1½″ x 6½″ rectangle

Letter:

    (D) two 1¾″ x 3″ rectangles

    (E) two 1¾″ x 6½″ rectangles

Use the DHST to attach the B squares to the E rectangle.

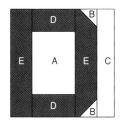 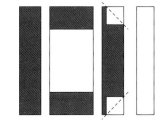

D, 6″ block

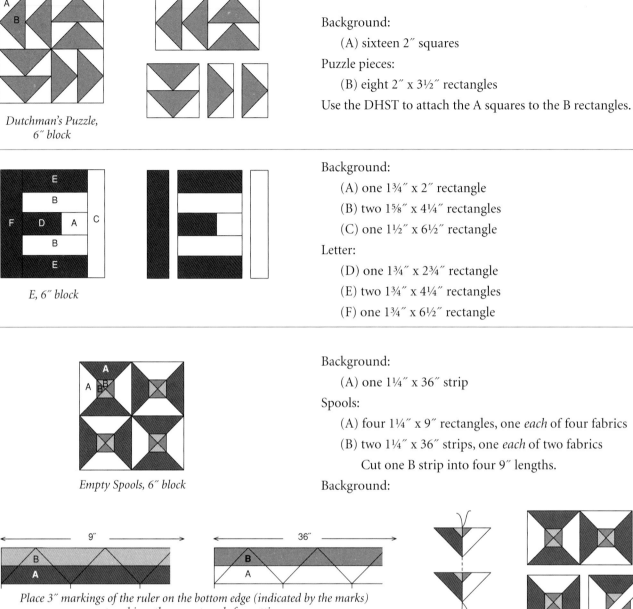

*Dutchman's Puzzle,
6″ block*

Background:

    (A) sixteen 2″ squares

Puzzle pieces:

    (B) eight 2″ x 3½″ rectangles

Use the DHST to attach the A squares to the B rectangles.

E, 6″ block

Background:

    (A) one 1¾″ x 2″ rectangle

    (B) two 1⅝″ x 4¼″ rectangles

    (C) one 1½″ x 6½″ rectangle

Letter:

    (D) one 1¾″ x 2¾″ rectangle

    (E) two 1¾″ x 4¼″ rectangles

    (F) one 1¾″ x 6½″ rectangle

Empty Spools, 6″ block

Background:

    (A) one 1¼″ x 36″ strip

Spools:

    (A) four 1¼″ x 9″ rectangles, one *each* of four fabrics

    (B) two 1¼″ x 36″ strips, one *each* of two fabrics

        Cut one B strip into four 9″ lengths.

Background:

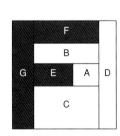

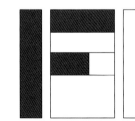

*Place 3″ markings of the ruler on the bottom edge (indicated by the marks)
to achieve the correct angle for cutting.*

F, 6″ block

Background:

    (A) one 1¾″ x 2″ rectangle

    (B) one 1⅝″ x 4¼″ rectangle

    (C) one 2⅞″ x 4¼″ rectangle

    (D) one 1½″ x 6½″ rectangle

Letter:

    (E) one 1¾″ x 2¾″ rectangle

    (F) one 1¾″ x 4¼″ rectangle

    (G) one 1¾″ x 6½″ rectangle

Background:

   (B) five 2⅜″ squares, cut in ***half diagonally***

Fox and Geese:

   (A) four 2″ squares

   (B) three 2⅜″ squares, cut in ***half diagonally***

   (C) one 3⅞″ square, cut in ***half diagonally***

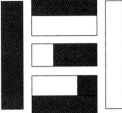

Fox and Geese, 6″ block

Background:

   (A) one 1¾″ square

   (B) one 1⅝″ x 3⅛″ rectangle

   (C) one 1⅝″ x 4¼″ rectangle

   (D) one 1½″ x 6½″ rectangle

Letter:

   (E) one 1⅝″ square

   (F) one 1¾″ x 3″ rectangle

   (G) two 1¾″ x 4¼″ rectangles

   (H) one 1¾″ x 6½″ rectangle

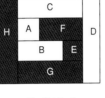

G, 6″ block

(A) one 3½″ square

(B) one 3⅞″ square, cut in ***half diagonally***

(C) one 6⅞″ square, cut in ***half diagonally***

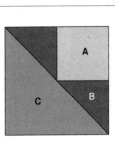

Grandmother's Choice,
6″ block

Background:

   (A) two 2⅞″ x 3″ rectangles

   (B) one 1½″ x 6½″ rectangle

Letter:

   (C) one 1¾″ x 3″ rectangle

   (D) two 1¾″ x 6½″ rectangles

H, 6″ block

Background:

   (A) four 1½″ squares

   (B) one 3⅞″ square, cut in ***half diagonally***

Heart:

   (C) two 3½″ squares

   (D) one 3⅞″ square, cut in ***half diagonally***

Use the DHST to attach the A squares to the C squares.

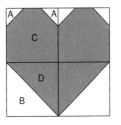

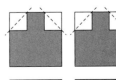

Heart, 6″ block

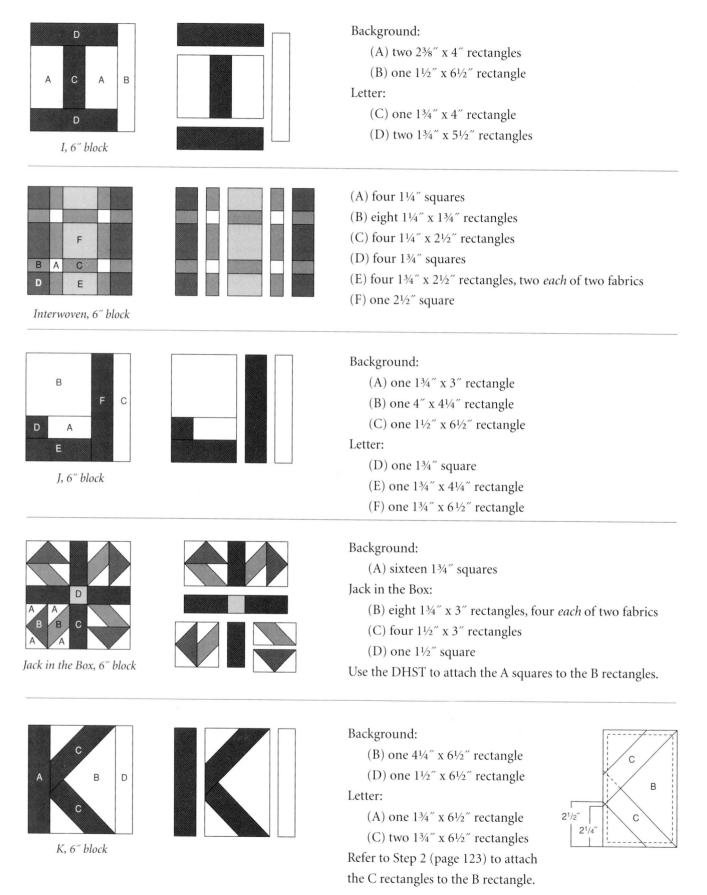

I, 6″ block

Background:
- (A) two 2⅜″ x 4″ rectangles
- (B) one 1½″ x 6½″ rectangle

Letter:
- (C) one 1¾″ x 4″ rectangle
- (D) two 1¾″ x 5½″ rectangles

Interwoven, 6″ block

- (A) four 1¼″ squares
- (B) eight 1¼″ x 1¾″ rectangles
- (C) four 1¼″ x 2½″ rectangles
- (D) four 1¾″ squares
- (E) four 1¾″ x 2½″ rectangles, two *each* of two fabrics
- (F) one 2½″ square

J, 6″ block

Background:
- (A) one 1¾″ x 3″ rectangle
- (B) one 4″ x 4¼″ rectangle
- (C) one 1½″ x 6½″ rectangle

Letter:
- (D) one 1¾″ square
- (E) one 1¾″ x 4¼″ rectangle
- (F) one 1¾″ x 6½″ rectangle

Jack in the Box, 6″ block

Background:
- (A) sixteen 1¾″ squares

Jack in the Box:
- (B) eight 1¾″ x 3″ rectangles, four *each* of two fabrics
- (C) four 1½″ x 3″ rectangles
- (D) one 1½″ square

Use the DHST to attach the A squares to the B rectangles.

K, 6″ block

Background:
- (B) one 4¼″ x 6½″ rectangle
- (D) one 1½″ x 6½″ rectangle

Letter:
- (A) one 1¾″ x 6½″ rectangle
- (C) two 1¾″ x 6½″ rectangles

Refer to Step 2 (page 123) to attach the C rectangles to the B rectangle.

Background:

    (A) one 6½˝ square

Handprint:

    (B) one 6˝ square

Refer to Part 2 (page 109) for help with appliqué, if needed.

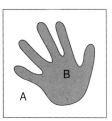 

Kid Print, 6˝ block

Background:

    (A) one 4¼˝ x 5¼˝ rectangle

    (B) one 1½˝ x 6½˝ rectangle

Letter:

    (C) one 1¾˝ x 4¼˝ rectangle

    (D) one 1¾˝ x 6½˝ rectangle

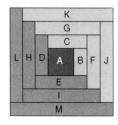

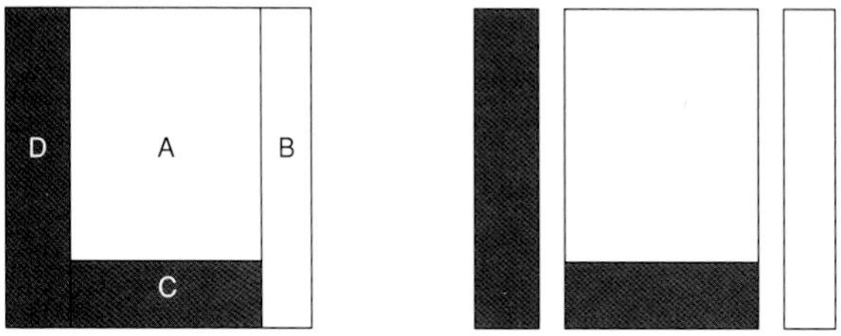

L, 6˝ block

Center:

    (A) one 2˝ square

Lights:

    (B) one 1¼˝ x 2˝ rectangle

    (C) one 1¼˝ x 2¾˝ rectangle

    (F) one 1¼˝ x 3½˝ rectangle

    (G) one 1¼˝ x 4¼˝ rectangle

    (J) one 1¼˝ x 5˝ rectangle

    (K) one 1¼˝ x 5¾˝ rectangle

Darks:

    (D) one 1¼˝ x 2¾˝ rectangle

    (E) one 1¼˝ x 3½˝ rectangle

    (H) one 1¼˝ x 4¼˝ rectangle

    (I) one 1¼˝ x 5˝ rectangle

    (L) one 1¼˝ x 5¾˝ rectangle

    (M) one 1¼˝ x 6½˝ rectangle

Sew the strips onto center A square, in sequence, from B to M, as shown.

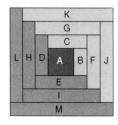 *[placed: Log Cabin diagram]*

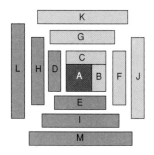

Log Cabin, 6˝ block

Background:

    (A) one 3˝ x 4˝ rectangle

    (B) two 1¾˝ squares

    (C) one 1¾˝ x 3˝ rectangle

    (E) one 1½˝ x 6½˝ rectangle

Letter:

    (B) two 1¾˝ squares

    (C) one 1¾˝ x 3˝ rectangle

    (D) two 1¾˝ x 6½˝ rectangles

Use the DHST to attach the B squares to the C rectangles.

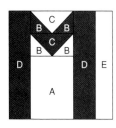 

M, 6˝ block

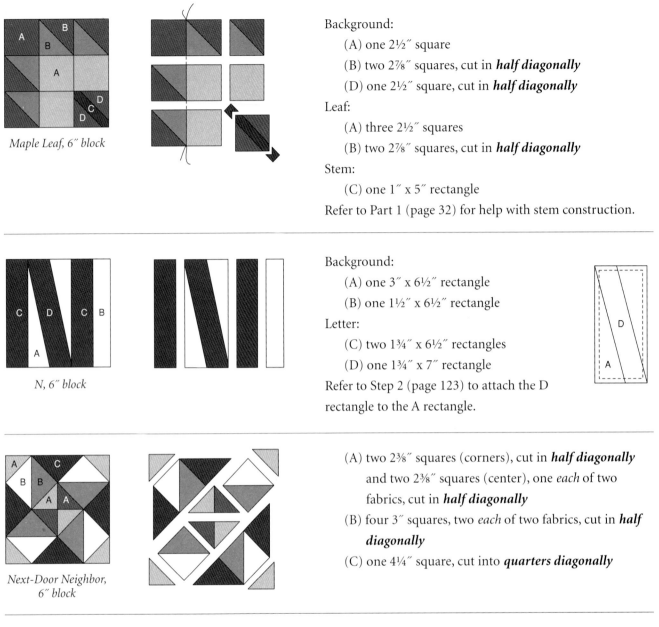

Maple Leaf, 6" block

Background:
  (A) one 2½" square
  (B) two 2⅞" squares, cut in *half diagonally*
  (D) one 2½" square, cut in *half diagonally*
Leaf:
  (A) three 2½" squares
  (B) two 2⅞" squares, cut in *half diagonally*
Stem:
  (C) one 1" x 5" rectangle
Refer to Part 1 (page 32) for help with stem construction.

N, 6" block

Background:
  (A) one 3" x 6½" rectangle
  (B) one 1½" x 6½" rectangle
Letter:
  (C) two 1¾" x 6½" rectangles
  (D) one 1¾" x 7" rectangle
Refer to Step 2 (page 123) to attach the D rectangle to the A rectangle.

Next-Door Neighbor, 6" block

  (A) two 2⅜" squares (corners), cut in *half diagonally* and two 2⅜" squares (center), one *each* of two fabrics, cut in *half diagonally*
  (B) four 3" squares, two *each* of two fabrics, cut in *half diagonally*
  (C) one 4¼" square, cut into *quarters diagonally*

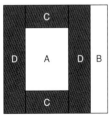

O, 6" block

Background:
  (A) one 3" x 4" rectangle
  (B) one 1½" x 6½" rectangle
Letter:
  (C) two 1¾" x 3" rectangles
  (D) two 1¾" x 6½" rectangles

Background:

    (A) four 2½″ squares

    (B) two 3¼″ squares, cut into **quarters diagonally**

Star points:

    (B) two 3¼″ squares, cut into **quarters diagonally**

Center:

    (C) one 2½″ square

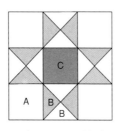
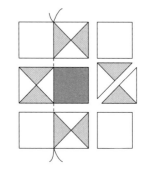

Ohio Star, 6″ block

Background:

    (A) one 1¾″ x 3″ rectangle

    (B) one 2¾″ x 4¼″ rectangle

    (C) one 1½″ x 6½″ rectangle

Letter:

    (D) one 1¾″ square

    (E) two 1¾″ x 4¼″ rectangles

    (F) one 1¾″ x 6½″ rectangle

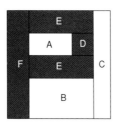
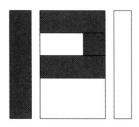

P, 6″ block

Background:

    (G) eight 1½″ squares

Pansy:

    (A) one 1½″ square

    (B) one 2½″ square

    (C) two 2½″ x 3½″ rectangles

    (D) one 3½″ square

    (E) two 1½″ x 2½″ rectangles

    (F) two 1½″ x 3½″ rectangles

    (H) two 1½″ squares

Use the DHST to attach the G squares to the B, C, D, and F

pieces, and the H squares to the E rectangles.

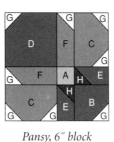

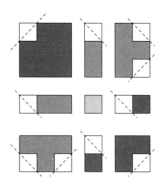

Pansy, 6″ block

Background:

    (A) one 3″ x 4″ rectangle

    (B) one 1½″ x 6½″ rectangle

Letter:

    (C) two 1¾″ x 3″ rectangles

    (D) two 1¾″ x 6½″ rectangles

    (E) one 1½″ square

Use the DHST to attach the E square to the B rectangle.

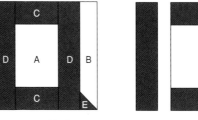

Q, 6″ block

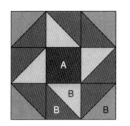

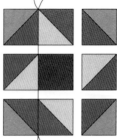

Quartered Star, 6″ block

(A) one 2½″ square

(B) eight 2⅞″ squares, two *each* of two fabrics *and* four of a third fabric, cut in ***half diagonally***

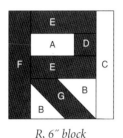

R, 6″ block

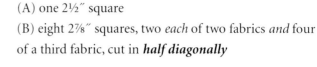

Background:

    (A) one 1¾″ x 3″ rectangle

    (B) one 2¾″ x 4¼″ rectangle

    (C) one 1½″ x 6½″ rectangle

Letter:

    (D) one 1¾″ square

    (E) two 1¾″ x 4¼″ rectangles

    (F) one 1¾″ x 6½″ rectangle

    (G) one 1¾″ x 5″ rectangle

Refer to Step 2 (page 123) to attach the G rectangle to the B rectangle.

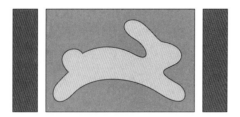

Rabbit, 6″ x 12″ block

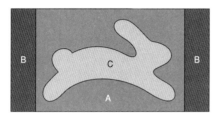

Background:

    (A) one 6½″ x 9½″ rectangle

Sides:

    (B) two 2″ x 6½″ rectangles

Rabbit:

    (C) one of template J (page 143)

Refer to Part 2 (page 109) for help with appliqué, if needed.

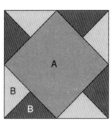

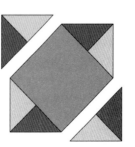

Right and Left, 6″ block

Right and Left:

    (A) one 4¾″ square

    (B) two 4¼″ squares, one *each* of two fabrics, cut into ***quarters diagonally***

Background:

    (A) two 1⅝″ x 4¼″ rectangles

    (B) one 1½″ x 6½″ rectangle

Letter:

    (C) two 1⅝″ x 1¾″ rectangles

    (D) three 1¾″ x 5½″ rectangles

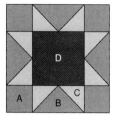
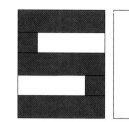

S, 6″ block

Background:

    (A) four 2″ squares

    (B) four 2″ x 3½″ rectangles

Star:

    (C) eight 2″ squares

    (D) one 3½″ square

Use the DHST to attach the C squares to the B rectangles.

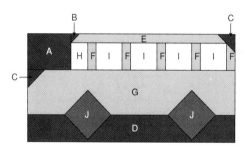
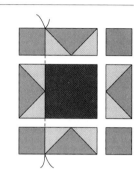

Sawtooth Star, 6″ block

Background:

    (A) one 2½″ x 3″ rectangle

    (B) one 1″ square

    (C) two 1½″ squares

Road:

    (D) one 2″ x 12½″ rectangle

Bus:

    (E) one 1″ x 10″ rectangle

    (F) five 1″ x 2″ rectangles

    (G) one 3″ x 12½″ rectangle

Windows:

    (H) one 1½″ x 2″ rectangle

    (I) four 2″ squares

Wheels:

    (J) two 2″ squares

Use the DHST to attach the B and C squares to the bus pieces. Refer to Part 1 (page 84) for help, if needed.

Schoolbus, 6″x 12″ block

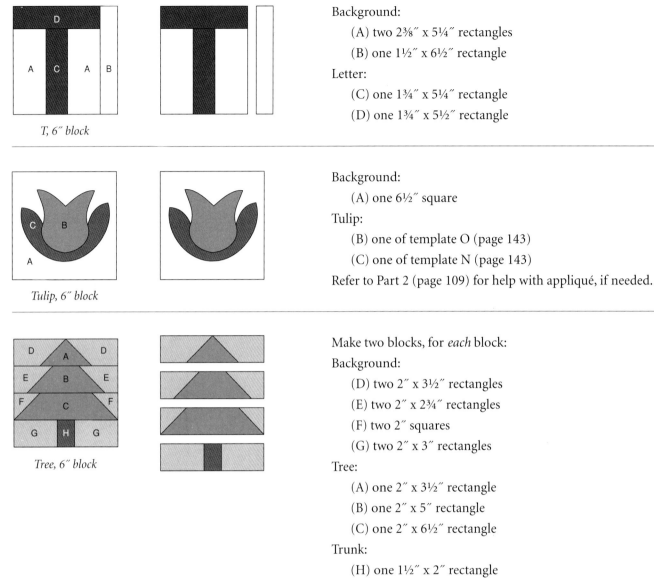

Background:

    (A) two 2⅜″ x 5¼″ rectangles

    (B) one 1½″ x 6½″ rectangle

Letter:

    (C) one 1¾″ x 5¼″ rectangle

    (D) one 1¾″ x 5½″ rectangle

T, 6″ block

Background:

    (A) one 6½″ square

Tulip:

    (B) one of template O (page 143)

    (C) one of template N (page 143)

Refer to Part 2 (page 109) for help with appliqué, if needed.

Tulip, 6″ block

Make two blocks, for *each* block:

Background:

    (D) two 2″ x 3½″ rectangles

    (E) two 2″ x 2¾″ rectangles

    (F) two 2″ squares

    (G) two 2″ x 3″ rectangles

Tree:

    (A) one 2″ x 3½″ rectangle

    (B) one 2″ x 5″ rectangle

    (C) one 2″ x 6½″ rectangle

Trunk:

    (H) one 1½″ x 2″ rectangle

Use the DHST to attach the background pieces to the tree pieces. Refer to Part 1 (page 48) for help, if needed.

Tree, 6″ block

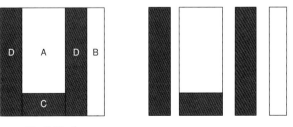

Background:

    (A) one 3″ x 5¼″ rectangle

    (B) one 1½″ x 6½″ rectangle

Letter:

    (C) one 1¾″ x 3″ rectangle

    (D) two 1¾″ x 6½″ rectangles

U, 6″ block

(A) two 1½″ x 13″ rectangles, one *each* of two fabrics

(B) one 2½″ square

(C) four 2⅞″ squares, two *each* of two fabrics, cut in **half diagonally**

Refer to Part 1 (page 12) for help with the Four-Patch block, if needed.

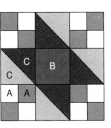
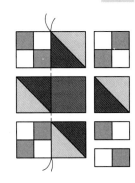

Underground Railroad, 6″ block

Background:

(A) one 5½″ x 6½″ rectangle

(B) one 1½″ x 6½″ rectangle

Letter:

(C) two 1¾″ x 8″ rectangles

Refer to Step 2 (page 123) to attach the C rectangles to the A rectangle.

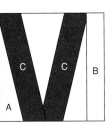

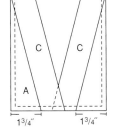

V, 6″ block

(A) five 2⅝″ squares, one of one fabric *and* four of a second fabric

(B) one 4½″ square, cut into **quarters diagonally**

(C) two 2½″ squares, cut in **half diagonally**

The B and C pieces are cut slightly too large to allow for straightening the block edges. Trim the excess.

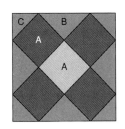
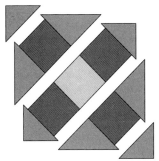

Vegetable Soup, 6″ block

Background:

(A) one 3″ x 4″ rectangle

(B) four 1¾″ squares

(C) one 1¾″ x 3″ rectangle

(D) one 1½″ x 6 ½″ rectangle

Letter:

(B) two 1¾″ squares

(C) one 1¾″ x 3″ rectangle

(E) two 1¾″ x 6½″ rectangles

Use the DHST to attach the B squares to the C rectangles.

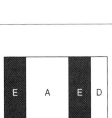
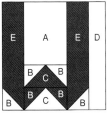

W, 6″ block

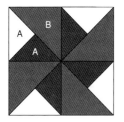

Whirlwind, 6″ block

(A) two 4¼″ squares, one *each* of two fabrics, cut into **quarters diagonally**

(B) two 3⅞″ squares, cut in **half diagonally**

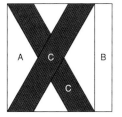

X, 6″ block

Background:

    (A) one 5½″ x 6½″ rectangle

    (B) one 1½″ x 6½″ rectangle

Letter:

    (C) two 1¾″ x 8½″ rectangles

Refer to Step 2 (page 123) to attach the C rectangles to the A rectangle.

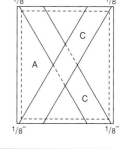

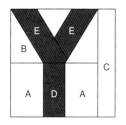

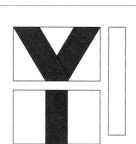

X-quisite, 6″ block

(A) eight 2″ squares

(B) four 3½″ squares

Use the DHST to attach the B squares to the A squares.

Y, 6″ block

Background:

    (A) two 2⅜″ x 3½″ rectangles

    (B) one 3½″ x 5½″ rectangle

    (C) one 1½″ x 6½″ rectangle

Letter:

    (D) one 1¾″ x 3½″ rectangle

    (E) two 1¾″ x 4½″ rectangles

Refer to Step 2 (page 123) to attach the E rectangles to the B rectangle.

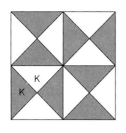

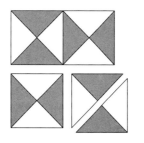

Yankee Puzzle, 6″ block

(K) four 4¼″ squares, two *each* of two fabrics, cut into **quarters diagonally**

Background:

    (A) one 4″ x 5½″ rectangle

    (B) one 1½″ x 6½″ rectangle

Letter:

    (C) one 1¾″ x 6½″ rectangle

    (D) two 1¾″ x 5½″ rectangles

Refer to Step 2 (page 123) to attach the C
rectangle to the A rectangle.

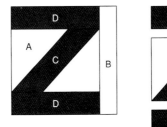 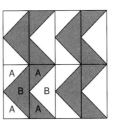 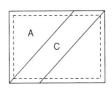

Z, 6″ block

Make three blocks, for *each* block:

Background:

    (A) eight 2″ squares

    (B) four 2″ x 3½″ rectangles

Zigzag:

    (A) eight 2″ squares, four *each* of two fabrics

    (B) four 2″ x 3½″ rectangles, two *each* of two fabrics

Use the DHST to attach the A squares to the B rectangles.

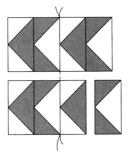

Zigzag, 6″ block

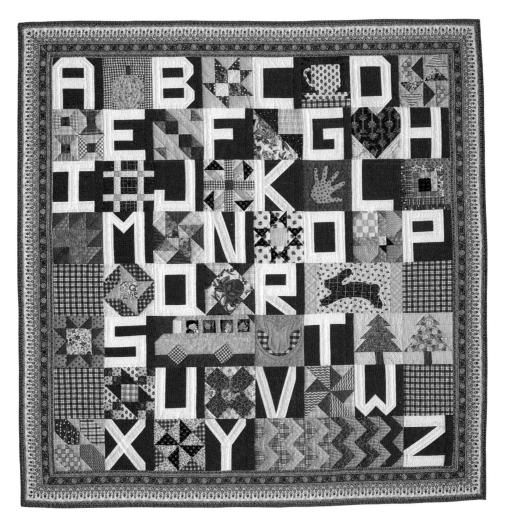

Alphabet Sampler by Katie Prindle; quilted by Anna Venti

Class Outline

Class One:
  Blocks: Letters C, E, F, G, H, I, J, and L

Class Two:
  Blocks: Letters A, B, D, O, P, Q, S, T, and U

Class Three:
  Blocks: Letters K, M, N, R, V, W, X, Y, and Z

Class Four:
  Technique: Quick Cutting
  Blocks: Grandmother's Choice, Ohio Star, Right and Left, Vegetable Soup, and Whirlwind

Class Five:
  Techniques: Strip Piecing and Half-Square Triangles
  Blocks: Fox and Geese, Interwoven, Log Cabin, Next-Door Neighbor, and Yankee Puzzle

Class Six:
  Technique: More Half-Square Triangles
  Blocks: Apple, Maple Leaf, Quartered Star, and Underground Railroad

Class Seven:
  Technique: Double Half-Square Triangles
  Blocks: Baby Bunting, Dutchman's Puzzle, Heart, Sawtooth Star, X-quisite, and Zigzag

Class Eight:
  Techniques: More Double Half-Square Triangles and Templates
  Blocks: Empty Spools, Jack in the Box, Pansy, and Tree

Class Nine:
  Technique: Appliqué
  Blocks: Cup and Saucer, Kid Print, Rabbit, Schoolbus, and Tulip

Class Ten:
  Techniques: Layering and Basting

Class Eleven:
  Techniques: Quilting and Binding

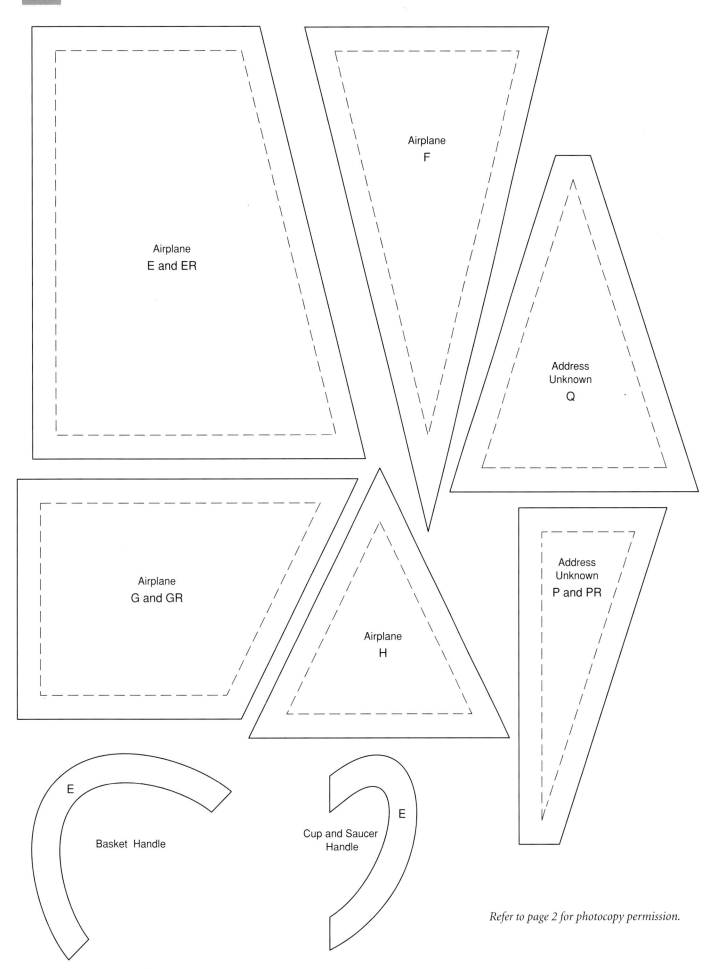

Airplane
F

Airplane
E and ER

Address
Unknown
Q

Airplane
G and GR

Airplane
H

Address
Unknown
P and PR

E

Basket Handle

Cup and Saucer
Handle

E

Optional leaves for appliqué

Blackbird:
Two and two reversed

Cherries

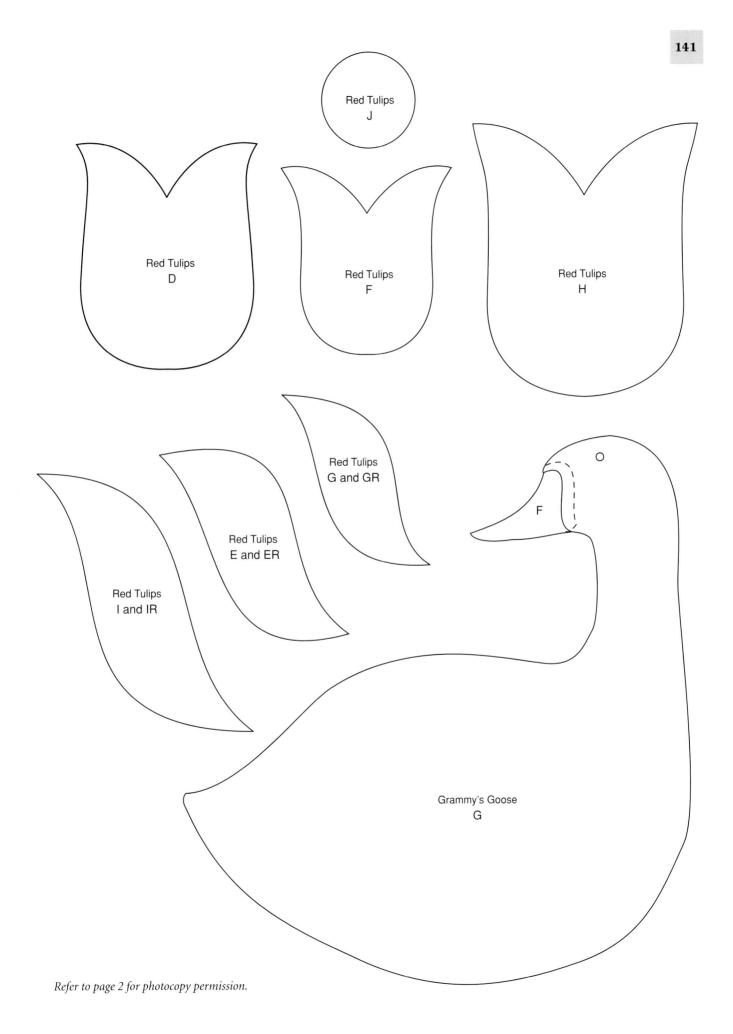

Red Tulips
J

Red Tulips
D

Red Tulips
F

Red Tulips
H

Red Tulips
G and GR

Red Tulips
E and ER

Red Tulips
I and IR

O

F

Grammy's Goose
G

142

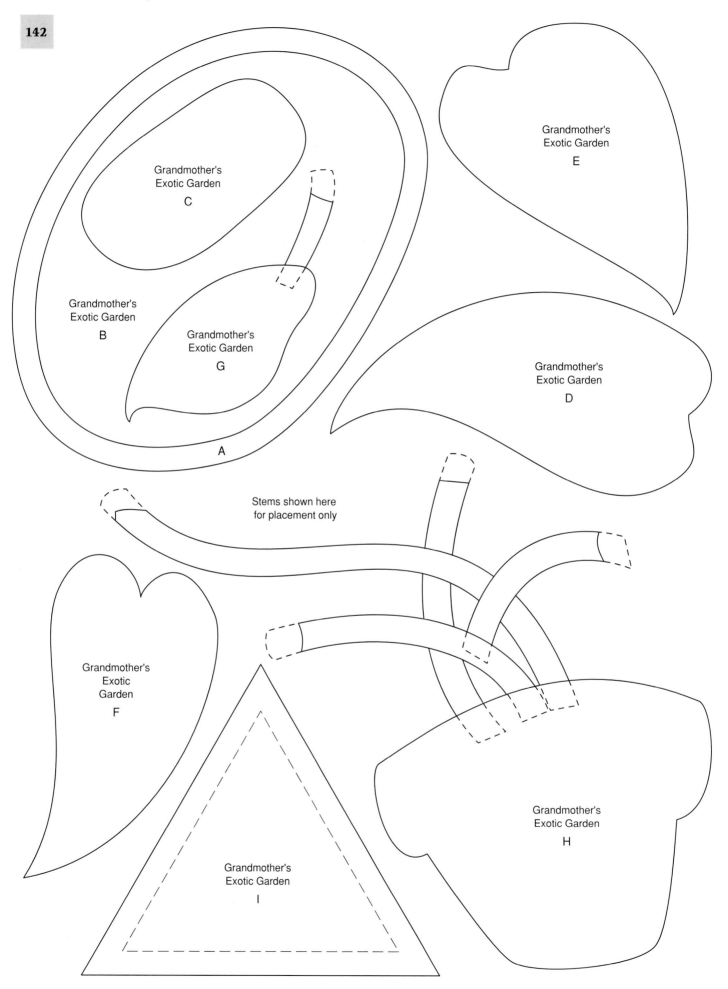

Grandmother's
Exotic Garden
C

Grandmother's
Exotic Garden
B

Grandmother's
Exotic Garden
G

A

Grandmother's
Exotic Garden
E

Grandmother's
Exotic Garden
D

Stems shown here
for placement only

Grandmother's
Exotic
Garden
F

Grandmother's
Exotic Garden
H

Grandmother's
Exotic Garden
I

Refer to page 2 for photocopy permission.

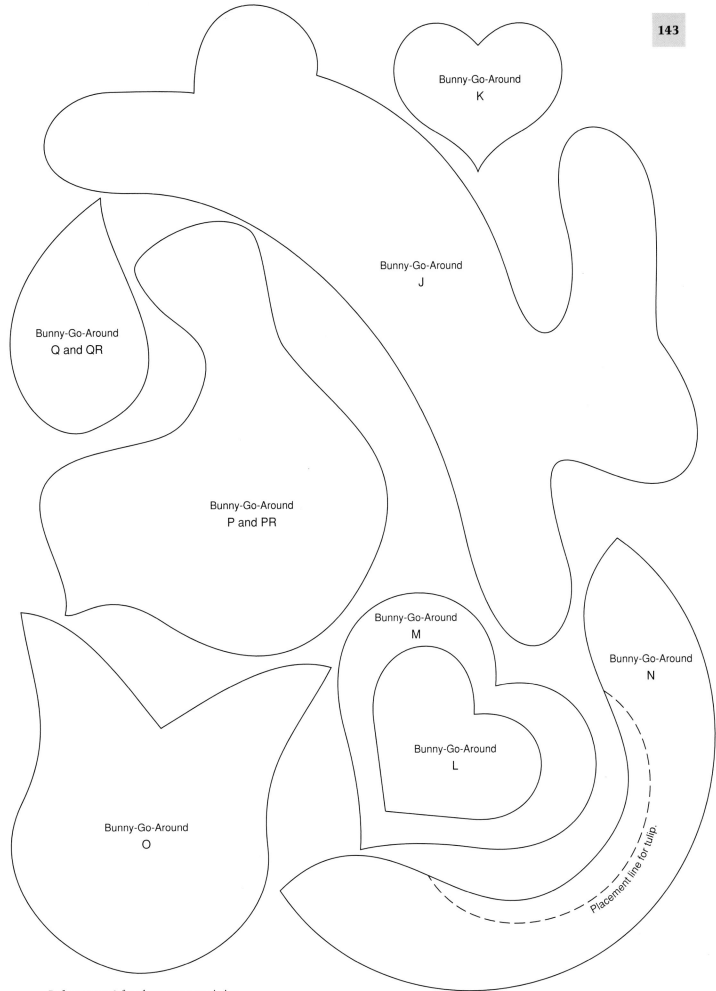

Bunny-Go-Around
K

Bunny-Go-Around
J

Bunny-Go-Around
Q and QR

Bunny-Go-Around
P and PR

Bunny-Go-Around
M

Bunny-Go-Around
N

Bunny-Go-Around
L

Bunny-Go-Around
O

Placement line for tulip.

Index

About the Authors

Diana McClun is one of the leaders in today's quiltmaking revival. When she owned a fabric shop, she taught quiltmaking to students who have now become outstanding and world-renowned quiltmakers, teachers, and authors in their own turn. One of the best known of these former students is Laura Nownes, with whom she has written three major instructional books. Together, in *Say It with Quilts*, these two celebrated authors share with you some of their favorite quilts and quiltmakers, and the heartwarming stories about each quilt, to evoke the simple pleasures that giving a quilt can bring to others.

For a complete list of other fine books, write to C&T Publishing, P.O. Box 1456, Lafayette, CA 94549